GETTING THE LOVE YOU WANT WORKBOOK

The New Couples' Study Guide

GETTING THE LOVE YOU WANT WORKBOOK

The New Couples' Study Guide

Harville Hendrix, Ph.D.

and

Helen LaKelly Hunt, Ph.D.

ATRIA BOOKS

NEW YORK   LONDON   TORONTO   SYDNEY

DISCLAIMER: This study guide is an *educational* process. While it is based on the theory and procedures of Imago Relationship Therapy, it is *not* therapy, and no therapeutic benefits are offered or implied. Therapy is a process that can occur only between a therapist and a couple. In this study guide, Imago Relationship Theory and Therapy procedures are modified to be educational.

If you and your partner experience difficulty with the exercises in this study guide, we encourage you to immediately consult an Imago Therapist or attend an Imago Couples' Workshop. You will find a list of therapists and workshops on the website imagorelationships.org, or you can call 800-729-1121 and ask for a referral.

ATRIA BOOKS
1230 Avenue of the Americas
New York, NY 10020

Copyright © 2003 by Harville Hendrix and Helen LaKelly Hunt

ISBN: 0-7434-8367-7

First Atria Books trade paperback edition December 2003

10   9   8   7

ATRIA BOOKS is a trademark of Simon & Schuster, Inc.

Manufactured in the United States of America

For information regarding special discounts for bulk purchases, please contact
Simon & Schuster Special Sales at 1-800-456-6798 or business@simonandschuster.com

Contents

We dedicate this workbook to the faculty of the Imago International Institute to honor them for their commitment to teaching Imago theory and practice worldwide. We especially thank them for their commitment to the highest teaching standards, their professionalism, and the joy of their colleagueship.

Faculty Instructors

Joyce Buckner, Ph.D.
Bruce Crapuchettes, Ph.D.
Maya Kollman, M.A.
Pat Love, Ed.D.
Sunny Shulkin, L.C.S.W.
Francine C. Beauvoir, Ph.D.
Maureen Brine, Reg.N., I.C.A.D.C.
Rick Brown, Th.M.
Nedra Fetterman, Ph.D.
Louis Getoff, Ph.D.
Wendy Palmer Patterson, M.S.W.
Kathleen Powell, M.S.W., L.C.S.W., B.C.D.
Hedy Schleifer, M.A.
Eugene Shelly, M.Div.
Mark Shulkin, M.D.
Rick Stolp, Ph.D.
Herb Tannenbaum, Ph.D.
Mike Borash, M.S. Ed.
Sophie Slade, Ph.D.
Jetta Simon, Clinical Psych.

The person who desires to see
the Living God face to face
should not seek God in the
empty firmament of the mind,
but in human love.

—*Dostoyevsky*

Introduction

PURPOSE OF *THE NEW COUPLES' STUDY GUIDE*

Getting the Love You Want introduced you to the "conscious marriage," a radically new understanding of marriage that fosters maximum psychological and spiritual growth. Such a marriage is created by becoming aware of and cooperating with the fundamental drives of the unconscious mind: to be safe, to be healed, to be whole. *Getting the Love You Want* also introduced you to Imago Relationship Therapy, the process designed to help you create a conscious marriage.

The New Couples' Study Guide is a unique twelve-week course designed to help you and your partner work through the exercises in Part III of *Getting the Love You Want*. This guide provides you with complete step-by-step instructions for transforming your relationship into a lasting source of love and companionship. It simulates the process you would participate in if you were to come to a Couples' Workshop or work with an Imago Relationship Therapist. Its purpose is to help you and your partner become aware of your unconscious agendas and show you how to intentionally cooperate with your unconscious to create a marriage that will satisfy your deepest needs.

Before beginning this study guide, please read all of *Getting the Love You Want* by Harville Hendrix, Ph.D. *The New Couples' Study Guide* is meant to be used in conjunction with *Getting the Love You Want,* as a companion to the exercises in Part III. It has been designed to build on the insights you gained about relationship and marriage from reading the book and contains only brief reviews of the book's content. Your successful participation in the process contained in this study guide will be greatly facilitated by having a complete understanding of Imago Relationship Theory and of the entire Imago Relationship process presented in *Getting the Love You Want.*

INTRODUCTION TO THE IMAGO PROCESS

When couples show up in Harville's office for counseling, they are often in a stew of anger, shock, despair, and sadness. Some are relative newlyweds, and they can't understand how they have plummeted from the heights of love and glory into a swamp of hopelessness and conflict. Others have been married for many years, and though they have been slogging along—in calm or in storm—and their days of wine and roses are a dim memory, they are no less devastated by the shambles of their marriage and the consequent lack of fulfillment in their lives. Even if life at home is relatively peaceful, couples lament that they have "nothing in common." And so they lead a disappointed or angry coexistence, each partner with his or her own friends and interests, in a marriage of convenience or an arrangement they endure "for the sake of the children."

They wonder if they will ever again feel love for their mates. Can they ever breach the chasm of silence or anger that has grown between them? Perhaps they should just cut their losses, they muse, and find someone who loves and understands them, someone who offers one more chance at the love and security they long for.

Whatever form they take, shattered dreams are painful. If you are considering using *The New Couples' Study Guide,* it is likely that you are also struggling to find love and meaning in your marriage. We assure you that there is hope. In fact, the pain and conflict of marriage arise not out of lack of love for your partners but from a misunderstanding of what marriage is about. Moreover, your conflict can be the fuel for the fulfillment you seek.

WHAT'S REALLY GOING ON IN RELATIONSHIPS?

Before you begin Session 1 of this study guide, we want to talk a little about what happens when we fall in—and out of—love. To make sense of what's really going on when couples fight, to gain insight into the hidden agenda of marriage, we need to look at the complex process of human growth and development and at how we human beings fit into the larger scheme of things.

We are creatures of nature, with the evolutionary program of our species encoded in our genes. We all begin life in a state of relaxed and joyful bliss, with a feeling of connectedness to everything and everyone. Our overwhelming impulse at birth is to sustain this feeling of connectedness, *to remain attached.* If our caretakers are attuned to our wants and needs, ready and able to provide warmth, safety, and sustenance, our feelings of aliveness and well-being are sustained. We remain whole.

But, of course, that's not the way it works out. Even in the best of circumstances, our parents are not able to maintain the perfect standards of our time in the womb, when everything was provided immediately and automatically in an atmosphere of total safety and continuity. Even the best parents are not available every minute, do not always understand exactly what is needed, and are unable to meet every demand. More to the point, most of our parents, hampered by their own nurturing deficits and beset by long-standing problems of their own, are unwilling or unable to meet our infant needs. Tired, angry, depressed, busy, ill, distracted, afraid, or sad, our parents fail to sustain our feelings of security and comfort.

But every unmet need causes fear and pain, and in our infantile ignorance, we have no idea how to stop the pain and restore our feeling of safety. Desperate to survive, we adopt primitive coping mechanisms. Depending on our temperament and the nature of our caretakers' neglect, our feeble defenses take many different forms. We may cry constantly to get attention. Alternatively, we may withdraw from the touch and attention of our neglectful caretakers, denying that we even *have* needs. Though we do what we can, already the world feels unsafe, and love is rationed.

THE ESCALATION OF LOSS AND DYSFUNCTION

Our impulse to remain attached is only the first in a programmed series of impulses that emerge as we grow. After the attachment stage, the need to explore emerges, and our mission changes accordingly: we need the freedom to move away from our caretakers and the reassurance that we can reliably return to them. Again, our ability to master this skill of exploration depends on how well our caretakers understand and support this new impulse. It also depends on how well our caretakers laid the foundation at the stage of attachment. If all goes well, the impulse to explore gives way to the impulse to establish a sense of identity, then competence, and on through concern and intimacy. Each stage builds on the last, forming the foundation on which new skills are built. Any impairment along the way compromises our ability to competently negotiate the next stage.

Meanwhile, throughout childhood, we are also being socialized, molded by our caretakers and communities to fit into society. We are told what to do, what to say, and how to behave. We see behavior modeled by friends, teachers, and TV characters, and we are intimate witnesses to the relationship modeled by our parents. Observant and malleable, we learn what to do to gain love and acceptance. Socialization, too, chips away at our sense of wholeness and safety, for, inevitably, we come to see that certain aspects of ourselves aren't working. These aspects may include the way we look or talk, the things that interest us, our abilities, or our attractiveness as boys or girls. In the interest, again, of survival, we repress or disown parts of us that society finds unacceptable or unlovable. Our sense of all-right-ness diminishes further, and we end up as shadows of our whole, true selves.

If you want evidence of this self-dismantling process, think about the young children you know. At two or three, most are still exuberant, lively, unique, and eccentric, though some may already show signs of apathy, anger, or fear that a deprived infancy has left in its wake. At eight or ten, the inhibitions are more obvious and numerous; it's the rare ten-year-old who is still unmistakably, unabashedly himself. By the mid-teens, the toll of incomplete nurturing and society's messages is seen in the rebellion, depression, or lack of self-esteem of inadequately loved teenagers.

To the degree that our caretakers, and our society, are able to support the emergence and solidification of our innate impulses, and to the degree that we are allowed to be ourselves, we survive and prosper. Most of us had "good enough" caretakers, and we do all right. Others of us didn't fare so well, and our lives are handicapped by our deep hurts. But all of us, to one degree or another, are nursing childhood wounds, coping as well as we can with the world and our relationships, using the feeble set of defenses born in the pain of childhood, along with parts of our true nature that we've stuffed into the drawers of our unconscious. We look grown up, we have jobs and responsibilities, but we are the walking wounded, trying desperately to live life fully, all the while unconsciously hoping somehow to restore the sense of joyful aliveness we started out with.

Falling in Love

When we fall in love, we believe we've found the bliss we were born with. Suddenly, we see life in Technicolor. We nibble each other's ears and tell each other *everything*. Our limitations and rigidities melt away. We're sexier, smarter, funnier, and more giving. We decide that we can't live without our beloved, for now we feel whole, we feel like *ourselves*. Finally, we feel safe and breathe a sigh of relieved deliverance. It looks as if everything is going to turn out all right, after all.

But inevitably—often when we marry or move in together—things just start to go wrong. In some cases, everything falls apart. The veil of illusion falls away, and it seems that our partners are different from what we thought they were. It turns out they have qualities that we can't bear. Even qualities we once admired grate on us. Old hurts are reactivated as we realize that our partners cannot or will not love and care for us as they promised. Our dream shatters.

Disillusionment turns to anger, fueled by fear that we won't survive without the love and safety that were within our grasp. Since our partners are no longer willingly giving us what we need, we change tactics, trying to maneuver our partners into caring—through anger, crying, withdrawal, shame, intimidation, and criticism—whatever works. We will *make* them love us, we think. Now we negotiate—for time, love, chores, gifts—measuring our success against an economic yardstick of profit and loss. The power struggle has begun, and it may go on for many years, until we split or settle into an uneasy truce, or until we seek help, desperate to feel alive and whole again, to have our dream back.

THE IMAGO EMERGES

What is going on here? Well, it looks as if you have found an Imago partner, someone, we're afraid, who is uniquely unqualified (at the moment) to give you the love you want. This is what's supposed to happen.

Let us explain. We all think that we have free choice when it comes to selecting our partners. In a way, we do. Ours was not an arranged marriage, after all, and there was no exchange of money or cows between our families. But regardless of what it is we think we're looking for, our unconscious has its own agenda when it comes to mate selection.

Our primitive old brain has a compelling, nonnegotiable drive to restore the feeling of aliveness and wholeness with which we came into the world. To accomplish that, it must repair the damage done in childhood as a result of needs not met, and the way it does that is to find a partner who can give us what our caretakers failed to provide.

You'd think, then, that we would choose someone who had what our caretakers lacked—and, of course, this is what we consciously seek. Would that it were that simple. But the old brain has a mind of its own, complete with its own checklist of desired qualities. It is carrying around an image of the perfect partner, a complex synthesis of qualities formed in reaction to the way our caretakers responded to our needs. Every pleasure or pain, every transaction of childhood, has left its mark on us, and these collective impressions form an unconscious picture we're always trying to match as we scan our environment for a suitable mate.

This image of "the person who can make me whole again" is what we call the *Imago*. Though we consciously seek only the positive traits, the negative traits of our caretakers are more indelibly imprinted in our Imago picture, because those are the traits that cause the wounds we now seek to heal. Our unconscious need is to have our feelings of aliveness and wholeness restored by someone who reminds us of our caretakers—in other words, someone with the same deficits of care and attention that hurt us in the first place.

So when we fall in love, when bells ring and the world seems altogether a better place, our old brain is telling us that we've found someone with whom we can complete our unfinished childhood business. Our imperfect caretakers, who have been freeze-dried in our memories of childhood, are reconstituted in our partner. Unfortunately, since we don't understand what's going on, we're shocked when the awful truth of our beloved surfaces, and our first impulse is to run screaming in the opposite direction.

And that's not all the bad news. Another powerful component of our Imago is that we also seek the qualities missing in ourselves—both good and bad—that got lost in the shuffle of socialization. If we are shy, we seek someone outgoing, and if we are disorganized, we are attracted to someone who is a neat freak. The anger we repressed because it was punished in our home, and which we unconsciously hate ourselves for feeling, shows up in our partner. But eventually, when our own feelings—our repressed exuberance, organizational skills, or anger—are stirred, we are uncomfortable, and we criticize our partners for being *too* outgoing, *too* organized, and *too* temperamental.

Waking Up to Reality

All of this seems to be a recipe for disaster, and for a long time this depressing state of affairs puzzled us. How can we resolve our childhood issues if our partners wound us in the same ways as our caretakers and we ourselves are stuck in childhood patterns that wound our partners?

Consciousness is the key; it changes everything. When we are unaware of the agenda of love, it *is* a disaster because our childhood scenarios inevitably repeat themselves with the same devastating consequences. There is a method to this madness, though. The unconscious re-creation of the ambience of childhood has the express purpose of bringing this old impasse to a resolution. When we understand that we have chosen our partners to heal certain wounds and that the healing of those wounds is the key to the end of longing, we have taken the first step on the journey to real love.

CONFLICT IS NATURAL

What we need to understand and accept is that conflict is supposed to happen. This is as nature intended it: everything in nature is in conflict. The truth is that the grounds for marriage are really based on incompatibility— it is the norm for relationships. Conflict needs to be understood as a given, a sign that the psyche is trying to survive, to get its needs met and become whole. It's only without this knowledge that conflict is destructive.

Ignorant of this process, our culture has made incompatibility the grounds for divorce, which counters nature's intention. Society has institutionalized permission for divorce out of a response to the childish wish for idealized, conflict-free relationships, which is a distortion of the natural process. Divorce does not solve the problems of marriage. We may get rid of our partners, but we keep our problems, carting them into the next relationship. Divorce is incompatible with the intentions of nature.

Romantic love is supposed to end. It is the glue that initially bonds two incompatible people together so that they will do what needs to be done to heal themselves and, in the process, heal the rifts in nature, of which we are an integral part. If we remain fixated on romantic love—"in love with love"—we remain stuck at the one-year-old stage of attachment. To restore our wholeness, our relationships need to grow successfully through all the developmental stages that were mishandled during childhood. The good news is that although many couples become hopelessly locked in the power struggle, it, too, is supposed to end. The emotional bond that is created by romantic love to keep partners together through the hard times evolves into an even more powerful organic bond through the process of resolving conflict.

The way we have come to see it is that nature is healing itself in our relationships. Each individual is a node of energy woven into the tapestry of being, and the tapestry is frayed and weakened where there is conflict. With our self-awareness, we humans do not have to remain stuck in childhood ruts. We are uniquely able to correct what has gone wrong. When we heal our relationships, we heal the rift in nature.

Making the Choice for a Conscious Marriage

A conscious marriage is not for the faint-hearted. It requires reclaiming the lost, repressed parts of ourselves, which we were told were dangerous to have and which we unconsciously hate ourselves for having. And it means learning more effective coping mechanisms than the crying, anger, or withdrawal that have become so habitual for us. In a conscious marriage, we change to give our partners what they need, no matter how difficult it is, no matter how much it goes against the grain of our personality and temperament. We stretch to become the person our partner needs us to be to heal. This is not easy, but it works.

Regardless of what we may believe, relationships are born not of love but of need. Real love is born *in* relationships, as a result of understanding what they are about and doing what is necessary to have them. You are already with your dream partner, but at the moment, he or she is in disguise—and, like you, in pain. A conscious marriage itself is the therapy you need to restore your sense of aliveness. The goal of your work in *The New Couples' Study Guide* is for you to extricate yourself from the power struggle and set yourself firmly on the path of real love.

How Will *The New Couples' Study Guide* Help You Begin to Create a Conscious Marriage?

In the work you and your partner will do together in this study guide, you will:

1. Tell each other about the wounds you received as a child.
2. Tell each other exactly what would make you feel loved.
3. Use that information to rechannel behavior into effective strategies

for loving and caring for each other, as well as for meeting personal needs.

4. Dismantle inappropriate beliefs from childhood.
5. Replace ineffective behaviors and defense strategies.
6. Rediscover the romance and the fun in your relationship.
7. Give your partner what he or she wants.

By redesigning your relationship to complete the unfinished business of childhood, you will achieve a conscious marriage. You will become whole, restoring your joyful aliveness. You will become passionate friends with your partner, developing what might be called *reality love,* which is based not on childhood notions of attachment but on knowledge, care, respect, and value of each other.

The Ground Rules

Let's look at some of the tools and processes you will use to achieve your conscious marriage. At the beginning of your first session, you will be asked to make the following commitments:

1. To complete all twelve sessions with your partner and to participate in those sessions actively and openly to the best of your ability.
2. To complete all between-session assignments.
3. To make no decision to terminate or continue your relationship until the completion of the twelve sessions.

Later on in the process, to help you meet the above commitments, you will be asked to make a *no-exit* decision, in which you spend time and energy that might be better spent on your marriage. For example, you will assess how often you attend PTA meetings, read, drink, watch TV, or sleep late, and you will even look at how much time you spend caring for your children. Then you and your partner will agree to cut out or reduce those diversions that are being used as an escape or an excuse not to be with each other. These diversions, or exits, are the ingredients of what we call the *invisible divorce,* and it's imperative to remove them so that you have enough energy to put into healing your relationship.

CREATING SAFETY

Your first two sessions will focus on creating a hospitable climate of willingness and openness to change in which to do your relationship work. You and your partner will create "Your Relationship Vision," in which you imagine the marriage you would like to have. This co-created vision will be a daily reminder to you of your goals. You will learn a new way of communicating and, most important, a new way of *listening* to each other that will become the backbone of your Study Guide process and your emerging conscious marriage.

In later sessions, you will learn new ways to say what is frustrating you and to ask for the behavior that you want instead. To remind you of the love you have felt for each other, you will be "Re-Romanticizing Your Relationship," giving each other special loving behaviors—with no strings attached and regardless of your current feelings about your partner—on a daily basis. These are target-specific behaviors; that is, they are exactly what your partner needs to feel loved and appreciated and safe. You will relearn to laugh and have fun together.

CHANGING THE WAY WE TALK, STRETCHING INTO NEW BEHAVIOR

Many couples' problems are rooted in misunderstood, manipulated, or avoided communications. To correct this, you will be introduced to "The Couple's Dialogue," the core skill of the Imago Process. Using this communications technique, you will restructure the way you talk to each other, so that what you say is mirrored back to you, validated, and empathized with. You will use the Couple's Dialogue to tell each other all about your childhood, to state your frustrations clearly, and to articulate exactly what you need from each other in order to heal. Clear communication is a window into the world of your partner, and truly being heard is a powerful aphrodisiac.

Then talk must be turned into action: we must give our partners what they need, and not just the easy stuff. Now we come to the heart of the matter: in a conscious marriage, we agree to change in order to give our partners what they need.

This is a radical idea. Conventional wisdom says that people don't change, and we should just learn to accept each other as we are. But without change, there is no growth, and we are resigned to our fate, to remaining stuck in our unhappiness.

Change is the catalyst for healing. In changing to give our partners what they need, we heal our own wounds. Our own behavior was born in response to our particular deprivations; it is our adaptation to loss. In giving our partners what is hardest for us to give, we have to bring our hidden selves out into the light, owning the traits we've repressed (rather than projecting them onto our partners) and enlivening atrophied parts of ourselves. When we change our behavior in response to our mates, we heal our partners and ourselves.

Here is an example of how this two-way healing works. Let's say that when your partner was a child, his or her mother was hospitalized and was unable to give your partner much emotional support when she returned home. In this situation, your partner might have developed a fear of being abandoned, attended by a fear of being ignored. These fears would have gone underground into the unconscious, only to be expressed outwardly as clutching, dependent, and attention-seeking behavior. Unless these behaviors were resolved later in childhood, they would show up in your relationship and be a source of irritation and frustration for you. As you came to know your partner's history through the Imago Process, you would understand that these behaviors, though triggered by something you might do, actually have their roots in your partner's childhood. Rather than feel angry or blame your partner, you would be more sympathetic.

But it would also be safe to assume that you have trouble dealing with this clutching or jealous behavior and that you can be emotionally distant and unsupportive of your partner. We could assume this because, according to Imago Process theory, your partner has an unconscious desire to change a person who is emotionally abandoning into a person who is emotionally close. One of the reasons your partner selected you is that you possess these required negative traits. Your own emotional distance is your way of coping with some childhood pain, perhaps caused by emotional smothering, and you naturally defend yourself against a recurrence of that experience. However, if you could see that your reaction serves no purpose in the present situation but instead is distancing you from your partner, you might be willing to drop this childhood defense and try a new approach that brings you closer together. Overcoming your fear and resistance to acting in this uncomfortable and unfamiliar way, you would grow to a new level of wholeness through accessing your denied affection and emotions. In the course of healing your partner's wound—the need for closeness—you would heal your own tendency to withdraw emotionally, and your partnership would transcend its former limitations.

RECLAIMING OURSELVES

Change rarely comes easily, and it requires great courage. Awakening traits long buried, traits both feared and hated, and learning new and uncomfortable behaviors can bring up tremendous anxiety. As long as we hate ourselves for having the repressed traits, we cannot believe that our partners can love us as we truly are. We are trapped in our own lies. But when we stop projecting our disowned traits—our anger or stinginess or sexual inhibition—onto our partners and take responsibility for them, we see that our partners can accept us as we are.

We call the process, by which we alter our entrenched behaviors to give our partners what they need, *Stretching,* for it requires that we conquer our fears, doing what comes *unnaturally* by moving beyond our accustomed beliefs and behaviors to access long-dormant parts of ourselves. Our resistance reflects our defenses. Often we feel that we're losing ourselves, but it's an illusion. We are not ourselves now; it is only in the crucible of change that we ever regain ourselves.

Over the course of time, as our partners demonstrate their love for us, as they learn about and accept our hidden selves, and as we stretch to love our partners, our pain and self-absorption diminish. We restore our empathic feelings for our partners and our feelings of connection to the other parts of ourselves that were lost in the pain of our childhoods. Finally, we learn to see our partners for themselves, with their own private worlds of personal meaning, their own ideas and dreams, and not merely as extensions of ourselves or as we wish they once were. We no longer say, "What, you liked that awful movie?" instead, we say, "Tell me why you liked that movie. I want to know how you think."

LEARNING TO LOVE

The barrier to love is self-hatred. When it breaks down, in the course of our dialogues with our partners, and in stretching to meet each other's needs, we see that we can be ourselves and still be loved. Finally, we can relax. Everything will be all right.

A conscious relationship has tremendous potential to correct the distortions of our caretaking and socialization. It is a spiritual path that leads us home again, to joy and aliveness, to the feeling of oneness we started out with. All through the process presented in *The New Couples' Study Guide,* you will be learning to express love as a daily behavior, in large and small ways. In stretching to give your partner what he or she needs, you learn to love. The transformation of your marriage will not be accomplished easily or quickly. Indeed, you are setting off on a lifelong journey—a journey that promises the ultimate reward of healing your relationship and yourself.

OVERVIEW OF *THE NEW COUPLES' STUDY GUIDE*

The study guide is organized into twelve sessions. Each session includes:

- *Review reading* from *Getting the Love You Want* and *The New Couples' Study Guide,* including relevant sections or chapters to review before the session.
- An approximate *time frame* for the entire session and also for the exercises within the session.
- A list of *objectives* for the session.
- An essay briefly explaining the *theory* behind the session and the rationale behind each exercise.
- Specific step-by-step instructions and work pages for completing the *exercises* and discussing them with your partner.
- *Points to remember* and *review questions* to reinforce your understanding of important ideas.
- *Between-session assignments* to help you integrate the knowledge and new skills into your daily life.

GUIDELINES FOR USING *THE NEW COUPLES' STUDY GUIDE*

Do no more than one session per week.

In order to fully integrate the learning from each session and maintain the momentum of the process, allow one week for each session. Changing a habit (that is, learning a new behavior) requires constant practice until the new behavior becomes more natural than the old. The time between sessions allows you to practice or continue to practice new behaviors during the week.

Each session should take approximately two hours to complete. (Specific times are noted at the beginning of each session.) The entire twelve-session process will take approximately three months.

Between-Session Assignments are as important as the sessions.

They help you use what you have learned on a daily basis in your relationship. When we learn something new, it is usually awkward and unfamiliar. Remember learning to ride a bicycle? Practice is what makes us good at it. The Between-Session Assignments are your practice time.

The Between-Session Assignments are separated into three categories:

- New assignments for the current week.
- Skills and behaviors you have already learned in previous sessions that you are asked to continue to practice and integrate into your relationship.
- Brief general reminders to help you continually integrate these skills and behaviors into your relationship.

By the time you arrive at the end of the study guide, most of your "work" will already be happening on a daily basis with your partner, and you will have begun the transformation into your conscious marriage.

Complete each session exactly as described and in the order presented. Only move on to a new session when all parts of the previous sessions are complete.

The exercises are sequential and build upon each other, following the principle of graduated change. You begin with an easy task first and move on to progressively more difficult ones. The learning in one exercise is a prerequisite for the learning in the next. Keep in mind that the more difficult a particular exercise seems to you, the more potential it contains for growth.

Set aside approximately two hours of uninterrupted time each week in a place where you can express yourselves freely.

Please note: exact times for each session are indicated at the beginning of the session. You may want to set a regular time each week for your sessions, or you may want to make an appointment for the following week after completing each session. Choose the arrangement that best supports your commitment to this process.

You will discover that doing the exercises requires a significant amount of time and commitment. You may need to hire a baby-sitter or reschedule some other activity to find the necessary time, just as you would if you were going to a weekly appointment with a therapist.

Have the following simple items available at every session:

- Two copies of *The New Couples' Study Guide.*
- A notebook or scrap paper to write on, if you wish, before you make entries into the study guide.
- Pens or pencils.
- A clock or watch.
- Tissues and water.

You will also need your copy (or two) of *Getting the Love You Want* in order to complete the review readings between sessions.

HOW TO PROCEED

Before beginning Session 1:

1. Read all of *Getting the Love You Want.*
2. Read the Introduction on the preceding pages.
3. Familiarize yourself with *The New Couples' Study Guide* by scanning the Contents or quickly scanning the whole guide.

SIMPLE SIX-STEP SESSION OUTLINE

BEFORE EACH SESSION:

1. Review relevant reading in *Getting the Love You Want.*

DURING EACH SESSION:

2. Read Objective and Theory sections.
3. Follow step-by-step instructions for doing the exercises and discussing them with your partner.
4. Review the session.
5. Make an appointment for the next session.

BETWEEN SESSIONS:

6. *Do* Between-Session Assignments.

A NOTE ABOUT EXERCISE INSTRUCTIONS

The instructions printed directly beneath the numbered steps state a simple action or task to be completed before moving on to the next numbered step.
    For example:

STEP 1.
On the worksheet, pages 25–26, write a series of short sentences that describe your personal vision of a deeply satisfying love relationship.

The bulleted sentences underneath these instructions elaborate upon the simple action or task of that step. The bullet items may describe in detail how to perform the action or task of that step, they may ask questions or provide hints or reminders to help you to complete the step, or they may refer you to completed sample exercise pages.

For example:

- Put each sentence on a separate line.
- Phrase all your sentences positively.

For example:	"We settle our differences peacefully."
Rather than:	"We don't fight."
Or:	"We trust each other."
Rather than:	"We don't get jealous."

- The questions below may help you focus on aspects of your ideal relationship that you may wish to include on your list:

  What do you feel toward each other?

  What do you do together?

  How do you relate to each other?

  Where do you live?

  What is your sex life like?

- There is a sample complete Relationship Vision on pages 31–32.

Occasionally, at the beginning of an exercise, there are notes or instructions about the exercise as a whole. These are marked with Δ.

For example:

Δ   **Do this exercise individually, and keep it secret from your partner.**

Your Relationship Vision

REVIEW in *Getting the Love You Want*
Pages 90–99; begin with the section "Becoming a Lover." On pages 113–114, read "Till Death Do Us Part."

TIME FRAME
Approximately 2 hours.

PART I: Commitment

OBJECTIVE

- Create safety and support for engaging in the Imago Process by establishing basic ground rules.

THEORY
The first step in the Imago Process is to establish some basic ground rules. You will be asked to complete all twelve sessions, to participate fully, and to make no decisions about ending or continuing your relationship until you have completed the entire process.

You are asked to make this commitment at the beginning of the process for a number of reasons. You are embarking upon a journey that will involve taking a good, deep look at yourself and changing yourself in order to create the changes you want in your relationship. Fear of change is basic to human nature. Being willing to risk making changes requires a certain amount of safety. Knowing that you and your partner will complete the entire process together helps create the safety you will need in order to let go of the familiar and venture into new territory, which is, at first, unfamiliar.

Fear of change brings up resistance. It is natural during this process for unconscious issues to emerge and for you to experience some anxiety. As we all know, a sure method for reducing anxiety is avoidance. You may find yourselves unable to find time to keep your appointments. You may find that as you do the more demanding exercises, you are tempted to put the book aside or alter the instructions. You may feel, "This isn't working. It's only making us feel worse. Let's stop." Many couples quit at this time. You will discover that if, at the outset, you make a strong commitment to finish all of the exercises and do them exactly as instructed, it will be easier to overcome your resistance to change.

Even if you are not sure you want to stay in your relationship, there are two reasons for asking you to commit fully to the relationship through the completion of the process. First, the problems you have in your current relationship are not about your partner. They reflect your own unresolved issues. Ending your relationship will not solve the problems of the relationship. You may get rid of your partner, but until you resolve your own issues, you will keep your problems, bringing them with you into future relationships. Second, you cannot know from here what your experience of yourself or your relationship will be at the end of this process. For example, you probably imagined as a teenager what it would be like to be a grown-up, but chances are that what you thought it would be like from a teenage point of view is not what you feel it to be now. You have changed and grown since your teenage years, and your perspective is different. Making no decisions until you have completed the twelve sessions allows you to change and grow and arrive in your new relationship before evaluating it.

Keep in mind that the information you gather in doing the exercises is designed to educate you and your partner about each other's needs. Sharing this information does not obligate you to meet those needs. Also, when you share your thoughts and feelings with each other, you become emotionally vulnerable. It is important that you use the information you gain about each other in a loving and helpful manner.

EXERCISE

Statement of Commitment

STEP 1.
Take a moment to yourself now to examine your priorities.

- How important to you is creating a more loving, supportive relationship?
- Are you willing to take part in a sometimes difficult process of self-growth?

STEP 2.
When you are ready, sign the Statement of Commitment in your book and your partner's book, indicating your willingness to participate.

STATEMENT OF COMMITMENT

I, _____, and my partner,

_____, agree to:

1. Complete all twelve sessions of the Imago Process together.
2. Complete all Between-Session Assignments.
3. Actively and openly participate in the entire process to the best of our abilities.
4. Make no decision to terminate or continue our relationship until the completion of all twelve sessions.

Signed _____

and _____

Date _____

PART II: Your Relationship Vision

OBJECTIVES

- Envision your personal ideal relationship.

- Co-create a shared vision for your relationship that inspires both you and your partner.

- Establish relationship goals that you and your partner can both support and work toward.

- Remind yourself of the potential in your relationship.

THEORY

A shared vision is essential to a successful relationship. "Where there is no vision, the people perish," says an ancient proverb. A vision provides direction and focuses your energy and efforts on a goal. Without a mutual vision, your relationship can become aimless and chaotic, and you will engage in random, stopgap behaviors to cope with your problems and conflicts. Defining your vision turns your energy away from past and present disappointments toward a more hopeful future, the future you want to create.

A vision is a view of the whole that influences the relationship of the parts. It gives direction to each decision and shapes each action. When conflicts arise, the resolution is determined by whether or not it is consistent with the relationship vision.

The relationship you now have is a creation of your separate desires and needs. It is a manifestation of your current unconscious vision of relationships. You and your partner are trying to bring your individual visions into reality, to your mutual frustration. Although these conflicting visions have their roots in the needs and desires of your childhood, you live them out in the present. They determine every thought, shape every action, and stimulate every feeling you have.

To have a successful relationship, you must co-create a shared vision as a conscious intention. A shared vision synthesizes separate dreams, desires, values, and needs. This joint creation becomes your conscious dream and your new reality. You may not be able to have the relationship of your private dreams, but you can co-create a new ideal relationship that will heal your childhood wounds and restore your original wholeness.

EXERCISE

My Relationship Vision

Suggested time: 30 minutes.

STEP 1.
On the worksheet provided, pages 25 and 26, write a series of short sentences that describe your personal vision of a deeply satisfying love relationship.

- Put each sentence on a separate line.

- Write each sentence in the present tense, as if it were already happening.

  For example: "We have fun together."

  "We have great sex."

  "We are loving parents."

  "We are affectionate with each other."

- Phrase all of your sentences positively.

  For example   "We settle our differences peacefully."

  Rather than: "We don't fight."

  Or: "We trust each other."

  Rather than: "We don't get jealous."

- Include both qualities already present in your relationship that you want to keep and qualities you wish you had.

- These questions may help you focus on aspects of your ideal relationship that you may wish to include on your list:

  What do you feel toward each other?

  What do you do together?

  How do you relate to each other?

  Where do you live?

  What is your sex life like?

  How do you play together?

What do you do with your free time?

How do you relate around work?

How do you relate around money?

What is the status of your children, if any?

How do you relate to your children, and how do they relate to you?

How do you relate to mutual friends and the opposite sex?

How are decisions made?

How do you handle conflict?

What is your relationship to in-laws or stepchildren?

How healthy are you physically?

MY RELATIONSHIP VISION

1 Similarities ✓	In my ideal love relationship:	2 Importance 1–5	3 Difficulty ✓

1 Similarities ✓	In my ideal love relationship:	2 Importance 1–5	3 Difficulty ✓

STEP 2.

Share your list with your partner, noting similarities.

- Place a check mark in column 1 next to the items that you have in common. It doesn't matter if you have used different words, as long as the general idea is the same.
- If your partner has written sentences that you agree with but did not think of yourself, add them to your list as you go, placing a check mark beside them in column 1.

STEP 3.

Working by yourself, in column 2 rank each sentence (including the ones that are not shared) with a number from 1 to 5 according to its importance to you.

- A 1 indicates "very important," and a 5 indicates "not so important."

STEP 4.

Working by yourself, in column 3 put a check mark beside those items that you think would be most difficult for the two of you to achieve.

EXERCISE

OUR MUTUAL RELATIONSHIP VISION
Suggested time: 30–45 minutes.

STEP 1.
On the worksheet on pages 29–30, create your Mutual Relationship Vision using sentences from both of your individual relationship vision lists.

- Record your Mutual Relationship Vision in *both* of your books. You will need two copies later.
- Begin with the items that you both agree are most important.
- At the bottom of the list, write items that you both agree are relatively unimportant.
- If there is an item that is a source of conflict between you, see if you can come up with a compromise statement that satisfies both of you. If not, leave the item off your combined list.
- As you create your shared vision, remember to write each sentence in the present tense, write each sentence positively, and write short, descriptive sentences.
- For guidance, a completed sample Mutual Relationship Vision follows.

STEP 2.
Record the importance, for both of you, of each item on your mutual list.

- Write your name at the top of column 1 on the left side of the page, and write your partner's name at the top of column 2 on the right side of the page.
- In column 1, under your name, fill in the number that reflects the importance of each item to you. As before, a 1 indicates "very important," and a 5 indicates "not so important."
- Have your partner do the same for himself or herself in column 2.

STEP 3.
In column 3 on the far right side of the page, put a check mark beside the sentences you both agree would be difficult to achieve.

STEP 4.
When you have finished co-creating your Mutual Relationship Vision, read it out loud to each other.

OUR MUTUAL RELATIONSHIP VISION

1 My name Importance 1–5	In my ideal love relationship:	2 Partner's name Importance 1–5	3 Mutual difficulty ✓

1 My name Importance 1–5	In my ideal love relationship:	2 Partner's name Importance 1–5	3 Mutual difficulty ✓

OUR MUTUAL RELATIONSHIP VISION
Sample

1 My name AMANDA Importance 1–5	In my ideal love relationship:	2 Partner's name BILL Importance 1–5	3 Mutual difficulty ✓
1	We have fun together regularly.	1	
1	We meet each other's deepest needs.	1	
1	We trust each other.	1	
1	We feel safe with each other.	1	
1	We have satisfying and beautiful sex.	1	
1	We are sexually and emotionally faithful.	1	
1	Our children are secure and happy.	1	
1	We enjoy each other.	1	
1	We are healthy and physically active.	1	
1	We both have satisfying careers.	1	
1	We share important decisions.	1	
1	We work well together as parents.	1	
1	We communicate our feelings openly.	2	✓
1	We are each other's best friend.	2	
2	We experience passion for each other.	1	✓

1 My name AMANDA Importance 1–5	In my ideal love relationship:	2 Partner's name BILL Importance 1–5	3 Mutual difficulty ✓
1	We are financially secure.	2	
1	We are growing together spiritually.	3	
3	We settle our differences peacefully.	1	
1	We show love daily.	3	
3	We have daily private time.	3	
4	We live close to our parents.	3	
5	We have similar political views.	3	
3	We take vacations alone twice a year.	5	✓

STEP 5.
Read the Points to Remember together now.

STEP 6.
Answer the Review Questions together, noting your answers in the spaces provided.

STEP 7.
Read the Between-Session Assignments together now.

STEP 8.
If you have not scheduled a regular time for your sessions, make an appointment for your next session now. (Note: Session 2 is 3 hours long.)

STEP 9.
Remove the Mutual Relationship Vision from *one* of your study guides, and post it where you can see it daily. Keep the other copy in its study guide.

POINTS TO REMEMBER

- The problems you have in your present relationship reflect your own unresolved issues.

- Fear of change is basic to human nature and brings up resistance to any change process.

- Making a firm commitment at the beginning of the process will help you overcome any potential resistance during the process.

- Your current relationship is a creation of your separate, conflicting desires and needs.

- A Mutual Relationship Vision is essential to the development of a successful, conscious marriage.

REVIEW QUESTIONS

How will the commitment you have made be helpful to you as you work through this process?

What is a Mutual Relationship Vision?

Why is a Mutual Relationship Vision important?

BETWEEN-SESSION ASSIGNMENTS

1. **Read your Mutual Relationship Vision together once a day.**
   What we focus on is what we will create. Reinforcing your co-created, inspiring vision regularly will remind you of what you want to create and will help you make the daily choices that will turn your vision into a reality.
2. **Review Chapter 9, "Increasing Your Knowledge of Yourself and Your Partner," in** *Getting the Love You Want* **before Session 2.**

Learning to Communicate: The Couple's Dialogue

REVIEW in *Getting the Love You Want*
Chapter 9, "Increasing Your Knowledge of Yourself and Your Partner."

TIME FRAME:
3 hours.

OBJECTIVES

- Create clear and effective communication between you and your partner.

- Deepen your understanding of your partner's point of view.

- Become more receptive to your partner's communication.

- Experience the joy of truly being heard and understood.

THEORY

Effective communication is essential to a good relationship. Good communication skills may not solve problems or resolve issues, but no problem can be solved, or issue resolved, without it.

Communication, defined as the verbal or nonverbal exchange of information, meaning, and feelings, covers every possible way we can interact with each other. We may communicate well or poorly, but we cannot *not* communicate. There is no relationship in which there is no communication. Effective communication occurs when a message sent by one partner is received by the other, as it is intended.

One of the most effective forms of communication in a committed love relationship is the *Couple's Dialogue,* which is the core skill of the Imago Process. You will use it in every session. With practice, it will become a habitual part of your everyday communication with your partner. The Couple's Dialogue involves three processes: Mirroring, Validation, and Empathy.

Mirroring is the process of accurately reflecting back the content of a message sent by your partner. The most common form of Mirroring is paraphrasing. To paraphrase is to state in your own words what the message your partner sent means to you. It indicates that you have heard and understood what your partner has said. Any response made before actually arriving at an accurate understanding of the meaning of your partner's message is actually not a response to your partner at all. It is a response to your own interpretation of your partner's message. Until a message is clearly received, you are responding to yourself, not to your partner. When you are Mirroring your partner, the sending and paraphrasing of the message are repeated until your partner affirms that you have clearly understood the message he or she sent.

Validation is a communication to the sending partner that the information being received and mirrored makes sense. It indicates that you can see the information from your partner's point of view and can accept that it has validity—that it is true for your partner. Validation is a temporary suspension or transcendence of your point of view and allows your partner's experience to have its own reality. Typical Validating phrases are:

"I can see that . . ."

"It makes sense to me that you would think or feel that . . ."

"I can understand that . . ."

Such phrases convey to your partner that his or her subjective experience is not crazy, that it has its own logic, and that it is a valid way of looking at things. To Validate your partner's message does not mean that you agree with his or her point of view or that it reflects your subjective experience. It merely recognizes the fact that in every situation, no objective view is possible. In any communication between two persons, there are always two points of view, and every report of any experience is an interpretation that is the truth for each person. The process of Mirroring and Validation affirms the other person and increases trust and closeness.

Empathy is the process of reflecting or imagining the feelings the sending partner is experiencing about the event or the situation being reported. This deep level of communication attempts to recognize, reach into, and, on some level, experience the emotions of the sending partner. Empathy allows both partners to transcend, perhaps for a moment, their separateness and to experience a genuine meeting. Such an experience has remarkable healing power.

A dialogue transaction may then sound as follows:

(Mirroring) "So, if I got it, when I don't look at you when you are talking to me, you think that I am uninterested in what you are saying.

(Validation) "I can understand that; it makes sense to me . . .

(Empathy) "and I can imagine that you would feel rejected and angry. That must be a terrible feeling."

A Couple's Dialogue is complete when both partners have played Sender and Receiver. (See sample on page 42.)

Being accurately heard and understood begins to heal the wounds of our childhood. We were wounded by parents, teachers, and relatives who told us, "You don't feel that," and "You don't think that." When our partners step out of this chorus of denial and say to us, "I understand that you really do feel and think that way," our entire being is validated. We no longer feel that we have to cut off parts of ourselves to be loved and accepted. We can begin to be the complex, multifaceted people that we really are and still find acceptance in the world.

EXERCISE

The Couple's Dialogue

Suggested time: 2 hours.

STEP 1.
With your partner, decide who will be the sender and who will be the receiver.

STEP 2.
Sender: Say a simple sentence that begins with the word *I* and describes a thought or feeling.

For example: "I woke up this morning and felt anxious about going to work."

- Receiver: If the sentence seems too complex, ask for simplification. For example: "Could you say that in fewer words?"
- Sender: If your partner asks for a more simple message, repeat your communication as concisely as possible.

    For example, if your initial communication was: "I was really thinking a lot about what was going to happen at work this morning when I woke up, and that upset my stomach, but I got up and went anyway."

    Your concise repetition might be: "I woke up this morning and felt anxious about going to work."

MIRRORING: Steps 3, 4, and 5

STEP 3.
Receiver: Once a clear and simple communication has been sent, paraphrase your partner's message and ask for clarification.

For example: "This morning, you woke up feeling that you would rather stay home than go to work. Did I get what you said and felt?"

- Asking for clarification is important, because it shows a willingness to try to understand.
- Do *not:*
    - Respond in any way with your own point of view.
    - Try to psychoanalyze your partner.

- In the beginning, as you are learning to mirror, if you find yourself sometimes repeating word for word exactly what your partner said, make sure you fully understand the message and are not simply playing parrot.

STEP 4.
Sender: If your partner has not completely and accurately paraphrased your communication, help clarify his or her understanding of what you said.

For example: "Not exactly. I woke up this morning wanting to go to work but dreading what was going to happen."

- Repeat Steps 3 and 4 until the Sender feels completely understood.

STEP 5.
Sender: Acknowledge that what you said, thought, and felt was accurately communicated.

For example: "Yes, I feel heard."

VALIDATION: Step 6

STEP 6.
Receiver: Once you have accurately heard and understood your partner, validate your partner's message.

For example: "I can see that."

                    "That makes sense to me."

                    "I get it."

- You are validating your partner's point of view, whether or not you agree with him or her.

EMPATHY: Step 7

STEP 7.
Receiver: Once you have validated your partner's message, empathize with your partner by imagining how your partner feels about the situation he or she is describing.

For example: "I can imagine how anxious you must have felt."

STEP 8.
Switch roles, and repeat Steps 2 through 7 to complete the Couple's Dialogue.

- New sender: In the typical course of conversation, your message would be your response to the previous sender's communication; see the sample Couple's Dialogue on page 42. If you have no response, send a message that describes your thoughts or feelings about something else.

STEP 9.
Continue practicing the Couple's Dialogue for 10 to 15 minutes until you are more comfortable with the process.

- If you like, use the Theory section of this session as a topic for communication.
- A Couple's Dialogue is complete when both partners have played Sender and Receiver at least once.
- This exercise may feel like an unnatural, cumbersome way of relating at first, but it is a good way to ensure accurate communication, and it will become second nature with practice.

As Receiver, your role is to:

Listen fully to your partner.

Accurately paraphrase your partner's communication.

Validate your partner's experience.

Empathize with your partner's feelings.

As Sender your role is to:

Make a simple initial communication.

Help your partner clarify his or her understanding of your communication.

Acknowledge your partner when she or he has understood you.

STEP 10.
Reread your Mutual Relationship Vision from Session 1. Spend approximately 30 minutes communicating some of your thoughts and feelings about it using the Couple's Dialogue: Mirroring, Validating, and Empathizing.

- Keep your initial communications simple.
- Include every step of the exercise. There is an outline of the Couple's Dialogue following to use as a simple guideline.

THE COUPLE'S DIALOGUE
Simple Guidelines

Refer to this outline as you continue to practice the Couple's Dialogue in your day-to-day communications.

1.	Sender:	Communicate a simple thought or feeling.
	Receiver:	Ask for simplification if the communication is too complicated.
	Sender:	Restate your communication as concisely as possible.

MIRRORING

2.	Receiver:	Paraphrase the sender's communication, and ask for clarification.
3.	Sender:	Help your partner to clarify his or her understanding of your communication. Repeat the paraphrasing and clarification process until the sender is satisfied.
4.	Sender:	Acknowledge the receiver's accurate understanding of your communication.

VALIDATION AND EMPATHY

5.	Receiver:	Validate your partner's communication, and Empathize with his or her feelings.

THE COUPLE'S DIALOGUE
Sample

Jill: *I didn't like it last night when you didn't want to hear about my new job.*

Evan: *Last night when I didn't listen to you, you felt bad. Is that correct?*

Jill: *Almost, yes. I felt hurt that you didn't want to hear about my new job.*

Evan: *Ah, you really wanted to tell me about your new job, and when I didn't listen, you felt hurt. Is that it?*

Jill: *Yes!*

Evan: *I can understand why you would feel hurt when I didn't want to hear about your new job. I can imagine it must have made you feel sad and frustrated not to be able to share that.*

Jill: *Yes.*

Evan: *For me, I was distracted with my own day at work and just needed a little time to think to myself before I could listen to you.*

Jill: *So last night, when I tried to tell you about my new job, you were still thinking about something that had happened at your office and weren't ready to listen to me yet. Is that what you meant?*

Evan: *Yes, almost. Also, I felt a little irritated to have my thought process interrupted.*

Jill: *Okay. So yesterday, when I tried to talk to you about my new job, you really needed a little more time to sort out your day, and you wanted me to go away and leave you alone. Is that closer?*

Evan: *Well, almost. You didn't have to go away and leave me alone forever, but I would have liked about five more minutes to finish what I was thinking about.*

Jill: *Okay. So last night, when I tried to talk to you about my new job, you felt a little irritated because you would have liked me to wait five minutes while you finished what you were thinking about and then tell you about my new job. How's that?*

Evan: *Yes!*

Jill: *That makes sense to me. I can imagine you would feel as if I wasn't being sensitive to you right then.*

STEP 11.

Read the points to remember now.

STEP 12.

Answer the review questions together, noting your answers in the spaces provided.

STEP 13.

Read the Between-Session Assignments together now.

STEP 14.

If you have not scheduled a regular time for your sessions, make an appointment for your next session now. (Note: Session 3 is 2 hours and 30 minutes long.)

POINTS TO REMEMBER

- You cannot *not* communicate. Whatever you do or say is a communication.

- Effective communication is essential to a good relationship.

- Any response made before arriving at an accurate understanding of the meaning of a communication is a response to your own interpretation of the communication.

- When we feel heard or understood, we become more receptive to hearing and understanding.

REVIEW QUESTIONS

What is an effective communication?

What is the difference between mirroring a communication and responding to a communication?

Why is it important to validate your partner's communication?

What effect does empathizing with your partner's communication have on your partner?

What are the benefits of using the Couple's Dialogue with your partner?

BETWEEN-SESSION ASSIGNMENTS

1. **During the next week, use the Couple's Dialogue with your partner at least once each day in your conversations. Play both Sender and Receiver at least once.**
   - Sender: If you want to send a message using the Couple's Dialogue, ask if now is a good time: "I would like to have a Couple's Dialogue. Is now okay?"
   - Receiver: It is the Receiver's job to grant a Couple's Dialogue ASAP, now if possible. If not now, set an appointment time so the Sender knows when he or she will be heard.
   - Most especially, use the Couple's Dialogue whenever you and your partner are in a conflict situation.
2. **Review Chapter 3, "Your Imago," in** *Getting the Love You Want* **before Session 3.**
3. **Continue to read your Mutual Relationship Vision out loud together at least once a week.**

Imago I: Revisiting Your Childhood

REVIEW in *Getting the Love You Want*
Chapter 3, "Your Imago."

TIME FRAME:
2 hours and 30 minutes. Note: This is a very full session. (See Between-Session Assignments.)

OBJECTIVES

• Clearly understand the concept of Imago.

• Construct your personal Imago.

• Identify the unconscious agenda you bring to your relationship from your childhood.

THEORY
A basic assumption of the Imago Process is that each of us carries an unconscious image of our ideal partner which we formed in childhood. This image, or Imago, powerfully influences the type of partner we select as adults, as well as how we relate to that partner.

Let us review the definition of Imago. The Imago is our internal, largely unconscious image of the perfect partner. This composite picture is a synthesis of all the positive and negative traits of our primary caretakers related to the satisfaction or frustration of our childhood needs. Our primary caretakers might include our parents, one or more siblings, or even a baby-sitter or close relative—anyone responsible for our care and upon whom we were dependent for our basic needs. Our Imago also includes parts of ourselves that we disowned in childhood because they were unacceptable to those upon whom our survival depended or to society. We will have a deeper look at these missing-self traits in a later session. For now, we will concentrate on the part of our Imago that is based upon the traits of our early caretakers.

Though the Imago is a picture of both the positive and negative traits of our caretakers, the negative traits carry the most weight in our attraction to a partner. This is because in our selection of a mate, we unconsciously seek to be healed. We seek to get our needs met that were not met in childhood. It would seem logical that we would choose partners who do *not* have the negative characteristics that so wounded us. However, the wounds caused by these negative traits are what we now seek to heal. In replicating these negative traits in our partner choice, our old brain is trying to re-create the conditions of our upbringing in order to correct them. It is attempting to return to the scene of our original frustrations in order to resolve our unfinished business with our primary caretakers. From the perspective of our old brain, we *must* get what we need from the person or persons from whom it should have come in the first place—or, failing that, from a reasonable facsimile. A partner who is (at the moment) uniquely *unqualified* to give us what we want provides us with a perfect opportunity to resolve our unfinished business.

If our partners are so perfect for us, why, then, are we so invariably frustrated with them? This is because we are only aware of the positive Imago traits in our attraction to our partners. The negative ones have been hidden in our unconscious. We become frustrated with our partners because we expect them to have only the positive traits. However, it is in the negative traits that our deepest healing lies.

To see how this works, let's look briefly at an example of a typical Imago match which demonstrates how unfinished childhood business influences an adult relationship:

Mary's mother was often critical and controlling. In a crisis, however, she became nurturing and even indulgent. While her father was emotionally detached and physically absent from his family most of the time, with male friends he would exhibit an infectious, childlike playfulness. Mary's unfinished business is to get a critical, controlling, and distant partner who is sometimes nurturing, indulgent, and playful to be always nurturing, indulgent, and playful.

Thus, as an adult, Mary is consciously attracted to a man who is nurturing, indulgent, and playful, the positive qualities of both parents. But he is also critical, controlling, and emotionally and physically distant. He is a blend of both the positive and negative traits of her parents.

Mary, however, wants her partner to be warm, supportive, and playful all the time. She complains that he is physically absent too much, that he is more playful and childlike with his male friends than with her, and that he seems emotionally detached when he is with her. On special occasions, when he does spend time with her and shows his deep affection, she is very happy and peaceful. She wishes the relationship were like this all the time.

However, she is always a little anxious during these good times because, unconsciously, she expects them to end. Inadvertently, she may even do something that ends the good times, thus re-creating her childhood situation. Then, in her frustration, she complains, withdraws, or gets sick, as she probably did when she was a child. This is an attempt to get her partner, who is now merged in her unconscious with her parents, to meet her needs.

The unconscious mind seems to have no sense of linear time. Our adult Imago match is, in the timeless unconscious, our early caretakers. Our unfinished business with our early caretakers becomes a compelling agenda with our adult partners. We unconsciously re-create our early childhood impasse with our partners whose negative traits are similar to those of our early caretakers. Because we are unaware of our agenda here, we struggle against it, but this unconscious re-creation has the express purpose of bringing our impasse to a resolution.

In this session, you will revisit your childhood using a series of Guided Visualizations to uncover the agenda hidden in your unconscious so that you can openly *cooperate* with it toward healing your childhood wounds and getting your deepest needs met.

A Few Hints about Guided Visualizations

- Everybody's internal life is unique, and the written instructions may not exactly fit with your experience. Complete each action to the best of your abilities, in whatever way works best for you.
- Whatever comes to you will be useful. Trust it, and just allow it to happen.
- You may be surprised by some of the thoughts or feelings that come to you. Trust them even if they do not make sense to your adult mind.
- If, in the middle of a Visualization, you find yourself distracted by something in the external world, just close your eyes, take a deep breath to relax again, and go back to where you were inside.
- If you find your mind wandering from the task at hand, open your eyes, and reread the action you are performing to focus yourself, once again. It may be time to move on to the next sentence.

EXERCISE

Revisit Your Childhood (Guided Visualization)
Suggested time: 30 minutes.

Δ   Read one sentence at a time. Complete the action described in that sentence, then move on to the next.

Δ   You may wish to do this exercise separately, reading to yourselves and moving at your own pace. Or you may wish to do it together, appointing one of you to read each sentence out loud while you pace yourselves together. Or you may wish to take turns, with one of you reading and the other doing the visualization. This last choice will lengthen the session by 30 minutes. If you choose this last option, establish some kind of signal for the person visualizing to give to the reader when he or she has completed the action of one sentence and is ready to move on to the next sentence.

STEP 1.
Read "A Few Hints About Guided Visualizations," on the previous page.

STEP 2.
Begin to relax your body and mind.

- Take a long, slow stretch from your head to your toes, making sure to stretch every part of your body. Let out a deep sigh.
- Settle comfortably into your chair.
- Breathe deeply ten times, becoming more relaxed with each breath.
- When you are ready, allow yourself to close your eyes and relax even more, as you continue to breathe deeply.

STEP 3.
As you become even more relaxed and peaceful, bring to mind your childhood home, the earliest home you can recall.

- Imagine yourself in your earliest home as the child you were then.
- Look around and see the house from your perspective as a child.
- Listen for a moment to the sounds you hear as a child in your home.
- Be aware of what you feel as a child as you begin to wander around your home.

STEP 4.

As you continue to wander around the house, begin to find the people who influenced you most deeply. Stop and visit with them.

- When you find the first important person, see him or her with new clarity.
- Note his or her positive and negative traits.
- Tell this important person that you enjoyed being with him or her.
- Tell this person what you wanted from him or her, but never got.
  Be sure to share all your feelings, including anger, fright, hurt, and sadness.
  In your fantasy, everyone you meet listens to you and is grateful for your insights.
- When you have said everything you need to say to this person, move on in the house, and find another person who influenced you deeply.
- Repeat this step until you have visited with all of your primary caretakers.
  You may need to go somewhere other than your house to find an important caretaker. If you do, effortlessly find yourself with this caretaker wherever he or she is, and repeat this step with that person as well.

STEP 5.

When you have spoken with all of your primary caretakers, open your eyes, and turn to the following exercises to record the information you have gathered.

EXERCISE

Constructing My Imago

Suggested time: 20 minutes.

Δ   The remaining exercises in this session are to be done separately, except for a brief sharing of the last exercise in the session.

STEP 1.

Using the information you gathered in your Visualization, in the top half of the circle on the worksheet on page 54, next to the letter A, record the positive traits of all of your early caretakers.

- Begin with the first caretaker you visited, then the second, and so on.
- Lump all of the positive traits of all of your caretakers together. It is not necessary to separate them.
- List your caretakers' traits as you recall them from childhood, not as they are today.
- Describe them with simple adjectives or phrases. For example: *kind, warm, intelligent, religious, creative, always there, enthusiastic, reliable.*
- If you need help remembering any of this information, close your eyes, take a deep breath, and see yourself in your childhood home with the caretaker you are focusing on. You will remember.

STEP 2.

In the bottom half of the circle next to the letter B, record the negative traits of your caretakers.

- Again, lump all the traits together, list them as you remember them from childhood, and describe them with simple adjectives or phrases.

STEP 3.

Circle the positive and negative traits that seem to affect you the most.

CONSTRUCTING MY IMAGO

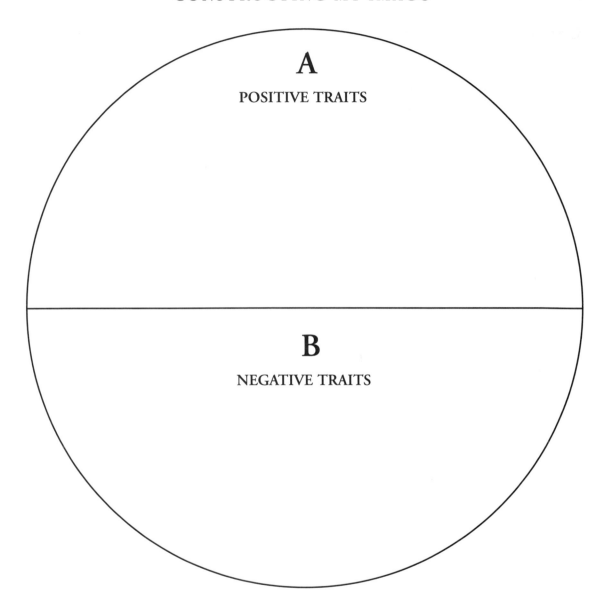

The sum of all positive and negative traits describes your Imago. The traits you circled are the most important.

EXERCISE

Positive Childhood Memories
Suggested time: 15 minutes.

STEP 1.
Close your eyes, take a deep breath, and center again on your early childhood home, briefly recalling the positive experiences you had with your caretakers.

STEP 2.
On the worksheet on page 56, in column 1, list the positive behaviors and experiences you remember with each caretaker from your childhood.

- Some of these may be repeats of the positive traits in the previous exercise.

STEP 3.
In column 2, under the letter C, list the most positive feelings you remember from your childhood with each caretaker.

- Feelings can be described with one word. For example: *happy, safe, loved.* If you are using more than one word, you are probably describing a thought.

POSITIVE CHILDHOOD MEMORIES

1 Positive behavior or experience	2 Positive feeling C

EXERCISE

Childhood Frustrations

Suggested time: 30 minutes.

△   See sample responses to Steps 1, 2, and 3 following the worksheet.

STEP 1.
Close your eyes, take a deep breath, and center again on your early childhood home, briefly recalling the negative experiences you had with your caretakers. On the worksheet on page 58, in column 1, list the recurring frustrations you remember with each of your caretakers.

> For example: "My mother was too protective."
>
>   "My father was gone a lot."

- Include any particularly painful events you remember with that person.
- Some of these may be repeats of the negative traits from your Imago construction.

STEP 2.
In column 2, under the letter D, list the negative feelings you experienced over and over again with each caretaker.

- First, bring to mind each caretaker in turn, and write the recurring negative feelings that come up associated with that caretaker.
- Then, look at each of the Frustrations you described, and write the negative feelings associated with each specific Frustration.
- Again, a feeling can be described with one word. For example: *angry, helpless, sad, anxious, afraid, disgusted.*

STEP 3.
In column 3, under the letter E, briefly describe the way you reacted to each Frustration.

- You may have reacted in more than one way. List all of your common reactions.

CHILDHOOD FRUSTRATIONS

	1 Frustration				2 Feeling D	3 Reaction E	
Mother							
Father							
Other							

CHILDHOOD FRUSTRATIONS
Sample

	1 Frustration	2 Feeling D	3 Reaction E
Mother	Always told me what to do.	Smothered	Withdrew/rebelled.
	My mother was overly protective.	Annoyed, smothered	I kept things to myself. Sometimes I was defiant
	My mother didn't really listen to me.	Sad, cheated	I talked loud. I sulked.
Father	My father was unavailable.	Tense	Pursuit/avoidance.
	My father was gone a lot.	Angry	Usually tried to please him.
	My father drank too much.	Anxious	Tried to ignore it. Sometimes would get stomach aches.
Other	My brother was a pest.	Hurt, lonely	
	I didn't get enough attention from my older brother.	Ignored, hurt	Kept trying to get his attention.
	I felt inferior to my older brother.	Devalued, helpless, angry	Resigned myself to my inferiority. Tried not to compete directly.

EXERCISE

My Deepest Unfulfilled Desires

Suggested time: 10 minutes.

STEP 1.

Once again, close your eyes, take a deep breath, and center on your early childhood home.

STEP 2.

Continue breathing deeply, and recall telling your childhood caretakers what you wanted from them and never got.

STEP 3.

Recall how you felt with each of your caretakers when you did not get what you wanted or needed.

STEP 4.

On the top of the worksheet on page 61, under the letter F, write your Deepest Unfulfilled Desires with each caretaker by completing the sentence: "What I needed from you most as a child and didn't get or didn't get enough of was . . ."

For example:

Mother: "What I needed from you most as a child and didn't get enough of was your undivided attention wholly focused on me; your support and acknowledgment for being big and strong as well as little and fragile; to be more special to you."

Father: "What I needed from you most as a child and didn't get enough of was your approval; your acceptance and approval of the parts of me that are different from you; more latitude to be different from you and still be 'okay'; you listening to me fully and patiently."

MY DEEPEST UNFULFILLED DESIRES

What I needed from you most as a child and didn't get or didn't get enough of was . . .

F

Mother	
Father	
Other	

EXERCISE

My Deepest Fears

Suggested time: 10 minutes.

STEP 1.

Close your eyes briefly, and, centering again on your childhood caretakers, one at a time, allow yourself to feel the deepest fears you had with each of them.

- The following list of common fears may help you identify your own. Fear of being:

neglected	ignored
abandoned	suppressed
rejected	disapproved of
smothered	controlled
shamed	devalued
made to feel guilty	unloved
invisible	found defective
excluded	depleted
ostracized	deprived
used	separate
dominated	

STEP 2.

On the worksheet on page 63, write the Deepest Fears you experienced with each caretaker.

MY DEEPEST FEARS

Mother	
Father	
Other	

EXERCISE

Unfinished Business—My Childhood Agenda
Suggested time: 20 minutes.

STEP 1.
On the worksheet on page 65, complete your Childhood Agenda using information from the preceding exercises in this session.

- The letter in parentheses indicates the location in the preceding forms of the information to be used to complete the sentences.
- Write the appropriate information in the spaces provided.

STEP 2.
Alternate reading your Childhood Agendas to each other.

- Read your agenda out loud to your partner.
- After you have heard your partner's agenda, acknowledge his or her communication by saying, "Thank you for telling me that."
- You are sharing your Childhood Agendas for information purposes only.
- Keep in mind that the information you gather is designed to educate you and your partner about each other's needs. Sharing this information does not obligate you to meet those needs. Also, when you share your thoughts and feelings with each other, you become emotionally vulnerable. It is important that you use the information you gain about each other in a loving and helpful manner.

MY CHILDHOOD AGENDA

I am trying to get a person who is (circled traits from B):

To always be (circled traits from A):

So that I can get (F):

And feel (C):

When I don't get (F):

I feel (D):

And I often respond by (E):

STEP 3.

Read the Points to Remember together now.

STEP 4.

Answer the Review Questions together, noting your answers in the spaces provided.

STEP 5.

Read the Between-Session Assignments together now.

STEP 6.

If you have not scheduled a regular time for your sessions, make an appointment for your next session now. (Note: Session 4 is approximately two hours long.)

POINTS TO REMEMBER

- The Imago is our old brain's picture of the perfect partner. This perfect partner is a synthesis of the positive and negative traits of our early caretakers, as well as traits of our own that we disowned in childhood in order to survive.

- The negative traits, which have been hidden in our unconscious, are the most potent part of our attraction to an Imago partner.

- Our deepest healing lies in getting someone with the negative traits of our early caretakers to give us what we needed and did not get in childhood.

- The unconscious mind has no sense of linear time. In our unconscious, our partner is our early caretakers.

- We re-create our childhood struggles with our Imago partner in order to bring them to a resolution and heal our wounds.

REVIEW QUESTIONS
What is the Imago?

Why are your partner's negative traits and behaviors so important?

Why is your partner a perfect match for you?

BETWEEN-SESSION ASSIGNMENTS

1. **This is a very full session. If you do not complete all of the exercises in the time you have allotted for the session, complete them as a Between-Session Assignment before Session 4.**
   - If you cannot complete all the exercises in one sitting, you can stretch this session over two weeks, thereby lengthening your twelve-week process to thirteen weeks.
2. **Review sections in the Introduction, starting with "The Imago Emerges" (see pages 5–6) and concluding with "Making the Choice for a Conscious Marriage" (see page 8) before Session 4.**
3. **Continue:**
   - Use the Couple's Dialogue at every opportunity. Allow it to become a habitual part of your communication with your partner, especially in times of conflict.
   - Reinforce your Mutual Relationship Vision by reading it together at least once this week before Session 4.

Imago II: Your Childhood Wound

REVIEW

Introduction, starting with "The Imago Emerges" (see pages 5–6) and concluding with "Making the Choice for a Conscious Marriage." (See page 8.)

TIME FRAME:

Approximately 2 hours.

OBJECTIVES

• Clarify your understanding of your Childhood Wound.

• Share your Childhood Wound with your partner.

• Deepen your understanding of and compassion for the wounded child inside your partner.

THEORY

In the womb, all of our needs are instantly and automatically taken care of. We are in a constant state of blissful fulfillment. But from the moment of birth, gratification of our needs is no longer automatic or instant. No matter how loving or well intentioned, our parents cannot possibly be available every minute, know exactly what we want all the time, and always meet our every need. Preoccupied with their own concerns and hampered by their own nurturing deficits from childhood, even the best parents are often unwilling or unable to meet their children's needs.

We are wounded when our nurturing needs are not met, and we are also wounded in the process of socialization, as we are trimmed and tailored to fit into society. We are taught that there are feelings and thoughts we cannot have and talents and aptitudes that are unacceptable. Our angry feelings and our sexual feelings, as well as other antisocial thoughts and feelings, get little support. Sometimes the invalidation is direct: we are told we *don't* think or feel or see what we *do;* we are directed not to be a certain way and to be another way instead. Sometimes the invalidation is indirect: our caretakers choose not to see or reward certain things. Subtly and overtly, we are given the message that only parts of us are acceptable. In essence, we learn that we cannot be whole and be acceptable in our culture.

Having been blissfully unaware before we were born of even having needs, we soon find we must *do* something in order to get our needs met. We learn that certain actions create a positive response from our caretakers, and we get what we want. Other actions cause a negative response from our caretakers, and we do *not* get what we want. In the interest of survival, we adapt our original being and take on the behaviors that get our needs met, while repressing the parts of ourselves that elicit negative response. Then, in reaction to our lack of adequate nurturing and in response to society's demands that we conform to its standards and to fill the void created by the repression of parts of ourselves, we erect a façade. If our caretakers weren't affectionate enough, we might become tough guys who don't need anything from anybody, or we might become fragile children, constantly in need of care. Our original, complete beings become deformed, chipped away at by inadequate nurturing and socialization.

Healing our childhood wounds is the prime directive of our unconscious and the underlying agenda in our lives. This is the agenda we bring to our partners, people whom our unconscious perceives as perfect re-creations of our early caretakers. Therefore, some of the most important information we can clarify for ourselves and share with our partners is a clear understanding of our wounds. Understanding the wounds that motivate unwanted feelings and behaviors in us enables us to have more compassion for ourselves. Understanding the wounded child who lies hidden behind behavior we find frustrating in our partners enables us to approach our partners with more compassion. Approaching our partners and ourselves with compassion helps up melt the impasse of our power struggle, the pattern of coercion and tit-for-tat scorekeeping we are locked in, where our unmet needs motivate a refusal to meet the needs of our partners and vice versa.

EXERCISE

My Childwood Wound

Suggested time: 1 hour.

Δ   This is a synthesis of the information you gathered in Session 3, along with any other information you can give your partner to help him or her clearly understand your Childhood Wound.

STEP 1.

On the worksheet on pages 72–73, describe your Childhood Wound so you can communicate it clearly to your partner in Step 2.

- A sample of this exercise follows the worksheet on page 74. The sample is fairly concise. As you are writing about your childhood wound, or as you are telling your partner about it, you may find yourself elaborating in much greater detail. We encourage you to do so.
- Describe your Deepest Fears in detail. (See worksheet in Session 3, page 63.)
    - Describe the incidents, if you remember them, that caused these fears.
    - Describe other incidents in your childhood that triggered (caused you to feel) these fears.
    - Describe what happens to you when your Deepest Fears get triggered.
- State your Deepest Unfulfilled Desires. (See worksheet in Session 3, page 61.) Describe in detail how you felt when your deepest desires were unfulfilled.
- Your responses to "Constructing My Imago," "Childhood Frustrations," and "My Childhood Agenda" may contain information you wish to include here also.
- Include any other information that will help you to describe your Childhood Wound to your partner.

STEP 2.

Share your Childhood Wound with your partner using the Couple's Dialogue.

- Determine who will be the Sender first and who will be the Receiver.
- Receiver: Hold your partner across your lap, as though cradling a child, while you Mirror, Validate, and Empathize with his or her communication.
- Sender: For 15 minutes, tell your partner about your Childhood Wound while she or he holds you and receives your communication. *Do not* just read what you wrote; tell your partner about it.
- This is a very important communication. If it takes longer than 15 minutes per person to fully communicate your wounds, take the extra time.
- Reverse roles, and repeat this step.

MY CHILDHOOD WOUND

MY CHILDHOOD WOUND
Sample

My deepest fear is of being unloved. That comes up around my mother and my father. Also fear of being disapproved of comes up with my father.

My mother's attention came and went when I was really young. She had a difficult pregnancy with my sister, and my sister, was born before I was a year old, so I didn't have her undivided attention for very long. Also, because I am the oldest child, I was always asked to put my needs for attention on the back burner to help meet the needs of my younger sisters and brothers. I learned how to protect myself when my mom got distracted and her love "went away." I learned how to feel unloved and still be okay—sort of, although I'm not really okay at all when I feel unloved. It is a cold and lonely feeling in my heart. When my fear of being unloved gets triggered, I panic. And I protect myself either by getting cold and hard and self-sufficient or by clinging like a pest, getting right in your face and needing you to tell me that you love me all the time. Either way, what I am really saying is, "Help! Please love me, please hold me, please pay attention to me and love me!!!"

With my dad, I had a fear of being unloved—some of which was about not getting enough attention because he worked a lot—but it was more as if his approval meant his love to me. He's a logical perfectionist, and I am an artistic, intuitive type. My fear of disapproval with him comes from my creative, artistic endeavors being received as "chaotic messes" and also because my thought process works so differently from his. I was always trying so hard to think like him, so I could do things "right" and please him. But, of course, no matter how hard I tried or how hard I thought about it, I could never do "right," because "right" to him meant the way he would do it, and he was the only one who could always do things his way and be "right" all the time. So I was always trying really hard and coming up wrong or not "right" enough. The hurt is that I could never please him enough—no matter how long or how hard or how carefully I thought about something. As a result, now, when I feel as if I'm being disapproved of, I either get mad because I have tried really hard and am not being appreciated for it, or I kick right into "You don't love me."

From my mom, what I wanted most was to be special—number one special to her, where I came first. Part of me thinks I'm bad to want that still—"What about everybody else? She's doing her best. I'm pretty much getting what everyone else is getting." But I feel as if I want more! I don't care if it's selfish. I just want to come first to somebody!

With my dad, I wanted his approval and his validation of my creativity—of my ability to think of new ways to see and do things. I still want his approval and validation for the fun, creative parts of me rather than his disapproval about how illogical or impractical I am. When he didn't approve of me or my actions, I felt as if he thought I was stupid or not good enough—couldn't do it right—couldn't think right. I felt really confused about how to be right in a logical, practical way for him. As if my feet had been grabbed out from under me and I didn't quite know how to stand.

EXERCISE

My Partner's Childhood Wound

Suggested time: 40 minutes.

STEP 1.
On the worksheet, pages 76–77, describe your Partner's Childhood Wound.

STEP 2.
Check your description of your partner's wound to see if it is accurate.

- Read your description of your partner's wound to him or her.
- Ask if it is accurate.
- Using the Couple's Dialogue, allow your partner to clarify your description of his or her wound until he or she feels that you clearly understand it.
- Reverse roles, and repeat this step.

MY PARTNER'S CHILDHOOD WOUND

EXERCISE

Re-Imaging Your Partner (Guided Visualization)
Suggested time: 25 minutes.

△   Read one sentence at a time. Complete the action described in that sentence, then move on to the next.

△   You can do this exercise separately, reading to yourselves and moving at your own pace; or you can do it together, reading each sentence out loud and pacing yourselves together; or you can take turns, with one of you reading and the other doing the visualization. This last choice will lengthen the session by 15 minutes. If you choose this last option, establish some kind of signal for the person visualizing to give to the reader when he or she has completed the action in one sentence and is ready to move on to the next sentence.

△   You may wish to review "A Few Hints About Guided Visualizations" in Session 3 on page 50.

STEP 1.
Begin to relax.

- Take a good stretch, and let out a deep sigh.
- Get comfortable in your chair.
- Breathe deeply a few times, becoming more relaxed with each breath.
- When you are ready, allow yourself to close your eyes and relax even more, as you continue to breathe deeply.

STEP 2.
Imagine yourself in a place where you feel totally safe and relaxed.

- This safe place may be a place that you have been in your life, or it may be a place that you create in your imagination just for today. It may not even be a place at all—it may be just an experience or a feeling of safety.
- Continue to breathe deeply and relax into your perfect, safe space.
- As you breathe, look around you, and notice what you see in your safe place. Take your time; notice details. Be aware of what you feel emotionally and physically. Be aware of anything you can touch or smell. Listen carefully to the sounds you hear in your safe space.

STEP 3.

As you continue to feel even more comfortable, safe, and relaxed, imagine your partner in your safe place with you.

STEP 4.

When your partner is in your safe space with you, imagine him or her as a wounded child.

- See your partner as a wounded child; remember what he or she has told you of how he or she was wounded.
- Allow yourself to listen with empathy to the sounds this wounded child makes.
- Let yourself feel your partner's pain. Feel your own empathic response.

STEP 5.

Imagine yourself holding and loving this child and healing his or her wounds.

STEP 6.

As you continue to hold and love your partner as a wounded child, allow your safe place to recede, and bring your awareness back to the room.

STEP 7.

Open your eyes, and look at your partner.

STEP 8.

Using the Couple's Dialogue, share the feelings you had about each other during the visualization.

STEP 9.

Read the Points to Remember together now.

STEP 10.

Answer the Review Questions together, noting your answers in the spaces provided.

STEP 11.

Read the Between-Session Assignments together now.

STEP 12.

If you have not scheduled a regular time for your sessions, make an appointment for your next session now. (Note: Session 5 is two hours long.)

POINTS TO REMEMBER

- Regardless of the best intentions of our caretakers, their inadequate nurturing wounded us.

- We were also wounded by repressive socialization (through our caretakers and the rest of society), which demanded that we conform to their standards and be other than our natural selves.

- Healing our Childhood Wound is the prime directive of our unconscious and the agenda that underlies our entire lives, especially with our Imago partners. If we want a satisfying relationship, this mutual healing *must* happen.

- Compassion for our partners' wounds will help us melt the impasse of the power struggle between us.

REVIEW QUESTIONS

What is socialization?

Why is it important to understand each other's Childhood Wounds?

BETWEEN-SESSION ASSIGNMENTS

1. **Review your partner's Childhood Wound several times this week.**

2. **Once a day, visualize yourself holding and loving your partner as a wounded child.**
   - Most important, if you are in a conflict situation with your partner, stop for a moment and visualize him or her as a wounded child.

3. **Review Chapter 4, "Romantic Love," and Chapter 5, "The Power Struggle," in** *Getting the Love You Want* **before Session 5.**

4. **Continue:**
   - Use the Couple's Dialogue whenever possible, allowing it to be a habitual part of your communication with your partner, especially in times of conflict.
   - Reinforce your Mutual Relationship Vision by reading it together at least once this week before Session 5.

Imago III: Discovering Your Unconscious Marriage

REVIEW in *Getting the Love You Want*
Chapter 4, "Romantic Love," and Chapter 5, "The Power Struggle."

TIME FRAME:
2 hours.

OBJECTIVES

- Understand the connection between your partner and your Imago.

- Identify how what you like and don't like about your partner reflects your Childhood Wound.

- Identify your Power Struggle with your partner.

THEORY
When we fall in love, we believe our deepest, most fundamental, most infantile yearnings are going to be satisfied. Our partners seem to have all the positive qualities we are looking for. They make us feel loved and taken care of as we were in the best of times with our childhood caretakers, when we did get what we wanted. Thrown into the bargain, our new partners also have positive qualities that we lack. For example, if we are serious and logical, our partners may be fun-loving and artistic. If we are shy about our sexuality, our partners may be sexually confident and comfortable.

As children, we repress or deny not only qualities that we may now perceive as negative (such as anger or neediness) but also qualities that we may now perceive as positive (such as artistic ability or intelligence) if these were criticized or unappreciated. Whether positive or negative, we needed to repress or deny these unacceptable parts of ourselves in order to fit in with our families and society, in order to survive.

The positive qualities, talents, or aptitudes we repressed are called the *lost self* (we explore the lost self in greater detail in Session 4). As adults, we choose partners who make up for these split-off parts of our being, whose complementary traits mirror the selves we have lost. At first, we perceive these complementary traits as positive, but as time passes, these positive qualities in our partners begin to wake up the same dormant qualities that have been criticized or forbidden in us. We become anxious and uncomfortable because our unconscious still regards these traits as taboo, as a threat to our survival.

In response to our discomfort around the complementary traits we once found so wonderful, we may find ourselves trying to repress our partners in the same way our caretakers repressed us. We have been projecting our own repressed positive traits onto our partners, and now we want to control those traits as they were controlled or repressed in us. Projection is taking disowned qualities that are incompatible with our self-image and attributing them to someone else: *"Oh, she's so expressive." "He's so organized." "She's so artistic." "He's so sexy."* Then, we may keep our projector running, switch reels, and begin to project the same traits in a negative light: *"She's emotionally excessive." "He's cold and unfeeling." "She won't get a real job." "He's a sex maniac."*

At about this time, our partners' negative traits (the negative traits of our early caretakers, of our Imago), the ones we so resolutely refused to see in the throes of romance and that our partners did their best not to show us at first, begin to become obvious. Not only have our partners become uncomfortable reminders of parts of ourselves that are not safe to have, but now they are reopening our Childhood Wounds, awakening our deepest fear, which at the core is an unconscious fear of death.

In response to the reinjury to our Childhood Wounds, we begin to have the familiar negative feelings and reactions we had to being frustrated in childhood. The Power Struggle has begun. Two of the three major sources of conflict in the Power Struggle have surfaced: we are stirring up each other's forbidden behaviors and feelings, and we are reinjuring each other's Childhood Wounds.

The third source of conflict surfaces when we begin to project our disowned *negative* traits onto our partners. Let's look at Bob's story as an example:

Bob grew up with a judgmental father who always wanted him to be perfect. He vowed over and over again never to be like his father. However, children learn by example. Like sponges, they soak up everything around them. Bob has a very judgmental streak, which he denies because he wants to be acceptable. Not only does he manifest this trait, although he is unwilling to acknowledge it, but one of the negative traits he unconsciously looks for in a partner is a judgmental nature, like his father's. As the veil of romantic love begins to lift, he begins to project his disowned judgment onto his partner, who is also judgmental but is now carrying a double load.

How can we recognize our own Power Struggle?

We know we are in the Power Struggle when we have the core fight we have had so many times that we know our parts by heart. We can find it when we hear ourselves or our partners using global words such as *never* or *always,* which indicate the wounded child at work, lost in the eternal now of childhood. We can recognize it when we criticize our partners for attributes we would never want to have or when our partners vehemently criticize us for something they deny in themselves.

The hope that fueled the excitement of our Romantic Love now becomes the expectation that fuels the frustration of our Power Struggle. In both Romantic Love and the Power Struggle, we are searching for a way to regain our original wholeness, and we believe our partners have the power to make us healthy and whole. But whereas in Romantic Love we perceive the possibility of being loved completely and forever by our partners, in the Power Struggle we perceive our partners as withholding love.

In the initial excitement of the possibility of getting all the love we want, we are willing to give our partners all the love they want. The Power Struggle sets in when we want delivery on that possibility of all the love we want, and we pull back, withholding love, to wait for it. When we feel love being withheld, we go into defense mode, protecting our wounds while at the same time still trying to get them healed. We go back to our familiar childhood frustration, feeling, and reaction patterns and begin to use our childhood tactics to get our needs met. Willing caretaking and cooperation become coercion, criticism, nagging, anger, withdrawal, and blame. These tactics invariably reinjure our partners' wounds. Although our goal is the same as it was during Romantic Love—to heal our Childhood Wound—we now find ourselves locked in a never-ending cycle of hurting our partners to get them to give us what we want and being hurt in return to get *us* to give them what they want.

Simply put, the hope that our needs will be met generates the ecstasy of Romantic Love, and the expectation that our needs will be met activates the frustration of the Power Struggle. In this session, you will gather the information you need to begin to unravel the dynamics of your own Power Struggle within your unconscious marriage and to escape from the romantic illusion of love with the movie star of your projections into the much more satisfying fulfillment of loving the real person who is your partner.

EXERCISE

Partner Profile

Suggested time: 20 minutes.

△   All of the exercises in this session are to be completed individually, except for the end
of the last exercise in the session.

STEP 1.
On the worksheet on page 87, in column 2, under the letter G, list the traits you like in
your partner.

- Include the traits that first attracted you to your partner.
- Use simple adjectives and phrases.

STEP 2.
In column 3, under the letter H, list the traits you don't like in your partner.

STEP 3.
Circle the positive and negative traits that seem to affect you the most.

STEP 4.
Compare your partner's traits with the traits of your Imago from Session 3.

- In columns 1 and 4, place a check mark next to the traits that are similar.

STEP 5.
Complete the sentences at the bottom of the worksheet, next to the letters I and J.

PARTNER PROFILE

1 Similar ✓	2 Positive Traits G	3 Negative Traits H	4 Similar ✓

I What I get from my partner that I enjoy the most (your most positive experiences):

_____

_____

_____

J What I want most from my partner and don't get or don't get enough of is (deepest frustrations) :

_____

_____

_____

EXERCISE

Frustrations with My Partner

Suggested time: 25 minutes.

STEP 1.

On the worksheet on pages 90–91, in column 2 under the letter K, list all of your partner's behaviors that you don't like.

For example: "You tell me I am stupid." "You don't talk to me after making love."

- Phrase your responses as if you are completing the sentence, "I don't like it when you . . ."
- Be succinct and specific.

STEP 2.

In column 3 under the letter L, write what you feel in response to each of the behaviors in column 2.

For example: "Angry and invalidated." "Hurt."

- Remember, a feeling can usually be described in one word.

STEP 3.

In column 4, under the letter M, describe your typical reaction to each of the behaviors you don't like.

For example: "Physically leaving the conversation." "Calling you names." "Withdrawing and being cold toward you."

- You are completing the phrase "And I react by . . ."
- You may react in more than one way. List all of your common reactions.

STEP 4.

In column 5, under the letter N, write the fear triggered by your partner's behaviors that you recorded in column 2, which you are protecting by reacting the way you described in column 4.

For example: "Being disapproved of." "Being unloved."

- You may want to refer to the list of fears and your responses to "My Deepest Fear" on page 63 in Session 3.
- A completed example of Steps 1 through 4 might look like this: "When you *don't talk to me after making love,* I feel *hurt,* and I react by *withdrawing and being cold toward you* to hide my fear *of being unloved.*"

STEP 5.

Review your list of Frustrations in column 2 to make sure you have included everything you can think of right now.

STEP 6.

In column 1, place a check mark next to the behavior/feeling/reaction patterns that seem to affect you the most.

FRUSTRATIONS WITH MY PARTNER

1 ✓ Affect me the most	2 Frustration K I don't like it when you . . .	3 Feeling L I feel . . .

4 Reaction M And I react by . . .	5 Fear N To hide my fear of . . .

EXERCISE

Behaviors I Like from My Partner

Suggested time: 15 minutes.

STEP 1.

On the worksheet on page 93, in column 2 under the letter O, list all of your partner's behaviors that you like. Be very specific.

> For example: "Kiss me goodbye in the morning."
>
>   "Save me cartoons from the paper that you like."

- You are completing the phrase, "I like it when you . . ."

STEP 2.

In column 3, under the letter P, write what you feel in response to each of the behaviors in column 2.

> For example: "Warm and loved." "Special."

- Remember, a feeling can usually be described in one word.

STEP 3.

In column 4, under the letter Q, describe your reaction to each of the behaviors in column 2.

> For example: "Feeling good about myself all day."
>
>   "Looking forward to seeing you when you come home."
>
>   "Wanting to do something special for you."

- You are completing the phrase "And I react by . . ."
- You may react in more than one way. List all of your common reactions.
- A completed example of Steps 1 through 3 might look like this: "When you *save me cartoons from the paper that you like,* I feel *special,* and I react by *wanting to do something special for you.*"

STEP 4.

In column 1, place a check mark next to the behavior/feeling/reaction patterns that you feel most strongly about.

BEHAVIORS I LIKE FROM MY PARTNER

1 ✓ Affect me the most	2 Behavior O I like it when you . . .	3 Feeling P I feel. . . .	4 Reaction Q And I react by. . . .

EXERCISE

Behaviors I Would Like from My Partner
Suggested time: 15 minutes.

STEP 1.
On the worksheeton page 95, in column 2, under the letter R, list behaviors you would like from your partner. Be very specific.

> For example: "Give me fifteen minutes of massage every day."
>
>   "Go food shopping with me once a month."

- You are completing the phrase, "I would like it if you would . . ."

STEP 2.
In column 3, under the letter S, write what you would feel in response to each of the behaviors in column 2.

> For example: "Relaxed and loved." "Supported and happy."

- Remember, a feeling can usually be described in one word.

STEP 3.
In column 4, under the letter T, describe what your reaction would be to each of the behaviors in column 2.

> For example: "Wanting to hear about your day."
>
>   "Having more energy to do things after work with you."
>
>   "Feeling excited to cook for you."

- You are completing the phrase "And I would react by . . ."
- A completed example of Steps 1 through 3 might look like this: "If you would *go food shopping with me once a month,* I would feel *supported and happy,* and I would react by *feeling excited to cook for you.*"

STEP 4.
In column 1, place a check mark next to the behavior/feeling/reaction patterns that would have the greatest effect on you.

BEHAVIORS I WOULD LIKE FROM MY PARTNER

1 ✓ Affect me the most	2 Behavior R I would like it if you would . . .	3 Feeling S I would feel . . .	4 Reaction T And I would react by . . .

EXERCISE

My Power Struggle with My Partner
Suggested time: 30 minutes.

STEP 1.
On the worksheet on pages 97–98, identify your power struggle with your partner by writing the appropriate information from the preceding exercises in the spaces provided.

- The letter and page number in parentheses indicate the location of the information to be used to complete the sentences.
- See the sample on page 99 following the worksheet.

STEP 2.
Alternate reading your Power Struggles aloud to each other.

- The sentences you have completed describe your unconscious marriage. The first and second sentences on page 97 describe the negative qualities and behaviors of your partner, with whom you reexperience your childhood feelings and the frustrations you had with your parents. The next five sentences describe the qualities and behaviors you need from your partner in order to heal your Childhood Wound and the feelings and behaviors you would have as a consequence of healing your Childhood Wound. The last seven sentences on page 98 describe the childhood feelings you reexperience when your childhood needs are not met with your partner and the adult version of the childhood behaviors you use to re-create your childhood situation.
- Remember, we are attracted to the negative qualities in our partners, and we re-create the frustrations of our childhood for the purpose of healing our Childhood Wounds.

STEP 3.
Spend about 15 minutes in a Couple's Dialogue sharing your feelings about what you have learned in this exercise.

- Keep in mind that the information you gather is designed to educate you and your partner about each other's needs. Sharing this information does not obligate you to meet those needs. Also, when you share your thoughts and feelings with each other, you become emotionally vulnerable. It is important that you use the information you gain about each other in a loving and helpful manner.
- The information you gather in this exercise may affect your behavior toward each other, and that is fine, but there is no obligation or agreement to change your behavior at this time.

MY POWER STRUGGLE WITH MY PARTNER

I am attracted to you and have chosen you because you are (circled traits from H, page 87):

And because you (check-marked behaviors from K, page 90):

I wish you would always be (circled traits from G, page 87):

And would always (check-marked behaviors from O, page 93 and R, page 95):

And especially would (I and J, page 87):

So that I would always feel (check-marked feelings from P, page 93 and S, page 95):

And would always (check-marked reactions from Q, page 93 and T, page 95):

When you (repeat K, previous page):

I feel (check-marked feelings from L, page 90):

And I react by (check-marked reactions from M, page 91):

To hide my fear of (check-marked fears from N, page 91):

When I (repeat M, above):

I cause you to react by (repeat K, above):

And being (repeat H, previous page):

MY POWER STRUGGLE WITH MY PARTNER
Sample

I am attracted to you and have chosen you because you are *sometimes distant, angry, controlling, and scary;*

and because you *sometimes withdraw from me when I need to be close, do not call when you are going to be late, get angry when I ask questions about where you have been, and do not consult with me when you make decisions that affect me.*

I wish you would always be *warm, close, accepting, and inclusive;*

and would always *spend more time with me, tell me about your loving feelings, include me in all decisions, and value my opinions;*

and especially would *initiate special occasions for us to be together;*

so that I would always feel *happy, safe, and cared about;*

and would always *want to be with you and nuzzle.*

When you *withdraw from me, don't call, try to control me with your anger, and make decisions that affect me without consulting me;*

I feel *alone and unsafe and depressed;*

and I react by *crying and withdrawing and visiting a friend who will listen to me;*

to hide my fear of *being abandoned and shamed.*

When I *cry, withdraw, and visit my friend for reassurance;*

I cause you to react by *getting angry, becoming distant, and excluding me;*

and being *distant, angry, and controlling.*

STEP 4.
Read the Points to Remember together now.

STEP 5.
Answer the Review Questions together, noting your answers in the spaces provided.

STEP 6.

Read the Between-Session Assignments together now.

STEP 7.

If you have not scheduled a regular time for your sessions, make an appointment for your next session now. (Note: Session 6 is 1 hour and 45 minutes long.)

POINTS TO REMEMBER

- Romantic Love and the Power Struggle are two sides of the same coin. The hope that our needs will be met generates the ecstasy of Romantic Love, and the failure to meet them activates the frustration of the Power Struggle.

- Not only are we attracted to our Imago partners because of the positive and negative traits of our early caretakers, but we are also attracted by repressed or disowned traits of our own that we annex or project onto our partners.

- Global words such as *never* and *always* let you know that the person is reacting out of his or her childhood wound.

REVIEW QUESTIONS

Why do we inevitably move out of Romantic Love into the Power Struggle?

What is projection? What is one quality that you may be projecting onto your partner?

Why do our feelings change so drastically about the qualities in our partners that we initially felt were such perfect complements to us?

BETWEEN-SESSION ASSIGNMENTS

1. Compare your responses to the exercises in this session with your responses to the exercises in Session 3.
2. Begin in the "Today You Pleased Me By . . ." exercise in the Appendix on pages 240–242. Write down three things every day that your partner does that you like. Share them at the end of each day. Keep track of the date in column 1.
   - Find three things you like every day, and share them with your partner regardless of how you feel about your partner.
3. Review Chapter 7, "Closing Your Exits," in *Getting the Love You Want* before Session 6.
4. Continue:
   - Visualize your partner as a wounded child, especially in conflict situations and when he or she behaves in ways that frustrate you.
   - Use the Couple's Dialogue as a habitual part of your communication with your partner, especially in times of conflict.
   - Read your Mutual Relationship Vision together at least once before Session 6.

Closing Your Exits

REVIEW in *Getting the Love You Want*
Chapter 7, "Closing Your Exits."

TIME FRAME:
1 hour and 45 minutes.

OBJECTIVES

- Identify the ways you avoid involvement with your partner.

- Begin gradually increasing the level of intimacy between you and your partner.

- Deepen your commitment to the process of creating a conscious marriage.

THEORY

In your sessions so far, you have been collecting information, gathering awareness about yourself and your partner. Now it is time to take action toward creating your Conscious Marriage. It is time to begin gradually making your unconscious wishes the conscious agenda of your partnership and making the changes that will bring you the love you want.

The first step in this process of change is to begin increasing your level of involvement with your partner by at first reducing and then eliminating the ways you avoid each other. In this session, you will identify and close your Exits. An Exit is any behavior or activity that avoids involvement in or drains energy from your relationship. Closing your Exits in this way serves two purposes. It allows you to increase your focus on the areas in your life, such as your relationship, that will bring you the most healing, and it creates a more secure environment in which to heal.

There are three categories of Exits. The diagram on page 107 visually represents these Exits. The first category, the Catastrophic Exits, are represented in the corners of the diagram. They are murder, suicide, divorce, and insanity. These Exits must obviously be closed, or there is no relationship to work on. The second category consists of Serious Exits: drug or alcohol abuse, affairs, and serious illness. Third are the Functional and Motivational Exits. They include ordinary, everyday activities such as work, child care, hobbies, and exercise. The activities or behaviors in this last category may not inherently be Exits, but when we use these activities to avoid intimacy with our partners, they become Exits.

When we avoid our partners and our relationships, we are essentially avoiding ourselves. As we have seen, the healing of our deepest wounds lies with our partners, our unconscious re-creation of our early caretakers. The more energy, in particular emotional energy, we have available to focus on our issues with our partners, the more effective we can be in resolving them. No matter how much we consciously think we would rather avoid the pain of feeling our issues, our unconscious has a nonnegotiable agenda to heal. We cannot heal something by ignoring it. Becoming more involved with our partners increases the possibility of creating positive and comprehensive change in our lives.

In order to make changes, we need to feel safe with our partners. As with most experiences in life, it is an interesting paradox that in order to create more safety in which to make changes, we must first take the scary step of making a change. Consciously cooperating with our internal need to be safe, to be healed, to become whole, and agreeing to remain within the boundary of our relationship by closing our Exits, allow us and our partners to experience a new sense of security. Then we can deal with our issues and conflicts without fear or danger of destroying our relationships.

You may feel some increased tension in yourself and your relationship as you close familiar Exits. Although you may feel at first that your relationship is becoming more difficult, the increased tension is a sign that you are focusing your energy where your real potential for healing lies, in the heart of your conflicts and wounds. You are engaging directly with your issues instead of ignoring or avoiding them. Increased discomfort is a sign that you are in unfamiliar territory, changing old, ineffective patterns of interacting with your partner.

In order to create effective change, we cannot simply eliminate an old habit; we must have a very specific, new habit to substitute for it. Creating effective change is a gradual, one-step-at-a-time process, with time between each step to integrate new behavior. Taking a path of least resistance here does not mean doing nothing—it means taking the step that is easiest to take next and keeping to your commitment to move forward. In this spirit, we suggest you begin by closing Exits that are easier for you to close.

EXERCISE

Identifying My Exits

Suggested time: 20 minutes.

STEP 1.

On the worksheet on page 108, in column 2, list all of the behaviors you use to exit your relationship.

- An Exit is any way you avoid being fully present with your partner.
- Include all of your ordinary, everyday Exits, such as "overeating," "staying late at work," "spending too much time with the children," "keeping separate bank accounts," "jogging ten miles a day," "watching TV," "not wanting to be touched," "avoiding eye contact."
- If you have trouble distinguishing an Exit from an essential activity or a valid form of recreation, ask yourself this question: "Is one of the reasons I'm doing this activity to avoid spending time with my partner?"
- Include any more Serious Exits, such as having an affair or using drugs.
- Remember, all of these behaviors are not, in and of themselves, Exits. They become Exits when you use them to avoid your partner.

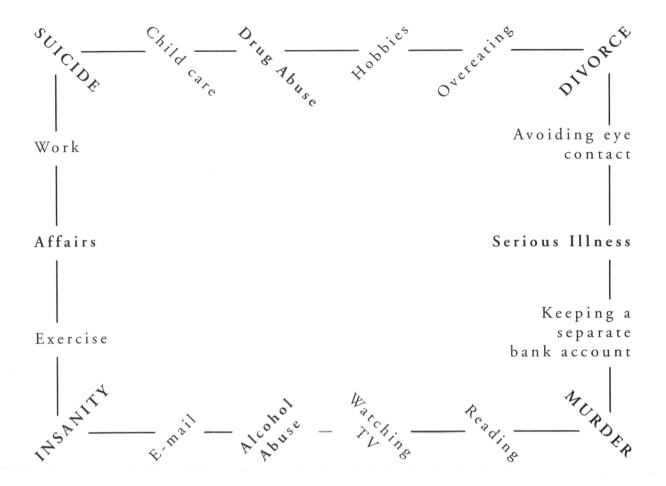

This perforated rectangle represents the boundary lines of most relationships. The open spaces are the Exits, all the ways partners avoid involvement with each other. The **CATA-STROPHIC EXITS** are indicated in each of the four corners, and **Serious Exits** are indicated in bold type. The rest of the Exits are examples of all the ordinary activities that become Exits when the motivation for doing them is, in part, to avoid spending time with each other.

IDENTIFYING MY EXITS

1 ✓ Willing to change	2 I avoid my partner by:	3 X Difficult to change

1 ✓ Willing to change	2 I avoid my partner by:	3 X Difficult to change

EXERCISE

Identifying My Partner's Exits

Suggested time: 45 minutes.

STEP 1.

On the worksheet on page 112, in column 2, list all of the behaviors you feel your partner uses to avoid involvement with you.

STEP 2.

Alternate reading your lists of your own Exits on pages 108–109 to each other.

- As your partner reads his or her own list, keep your study guide open to *your* list of your partner's Exits.
- Keep track of the Exits that your partner mentions that you also have on your list by placing a check mark in column 1.

STEP 3.

Choose one of you to be the Sender and one to be the Receiver first.

- You will be using an adaptation of the Couple's Dialogue to share the Exits that your partner did not mention for himself or herself.
- There is a sample of a modified Couple's Dialogue transaction for this exercise following the worksheet on page 113.

STEP 4.

Sender: Acknowledge the Exits your partner mentioned that you also listed.

For example: "Thank you for mentioning playing golf. I had that on my list, too."

STEP 5.

Sender: Read the unmentioned Exits, one at a time.

STEP 6.

Receiver: Use Mirroring to clarify your understanding of each additional Exit that your partner feels you use, and record each additional Exit on your Exit list.

- End each Mirroring transaction with a Validation. For example: "Thank you. I can see how that might feel like an Exit to you."
- It is not necessary in this exercise to empathize with each of your partner's suggestions.
- Add each Exit to your Exit list on pages 108 and 109 as it is clarified.
- Add every Exit your partner feels you use, whether you agree with it or not.
- If you strongly disagree that you use this behavior in any way to avoid your partner, write it at the bottom of the list on page 109.

STEP 7.
Repeat Steps 5 and 6 until all of the Sender's additional Exits have been clarified and included on the Receiver's list.

STEP 8.
Reverse the roles of Sender and Receiver, and repeat Steps 4, 5, and 6.

IDENTIFYING MY PARTNER'S EXITS

1 ✓ Similar	2 My partner avoids me by:

MODIFIED COUPLE'S DIALOGUE TRANSACTION FOR IDENTIFYING EXITS
Sample

Andrew: *Thank you for mentioning talking to your mom, bringing Tom and Dinah along with us on dates, and reading romance novels. I had them on my list, too. One Exit that you didn't mention was your watercolor painting. I feel you use that as a way not to spend time with me.*

Jennifer: *You think I paint to get away from you. Is that correct?*

Andrew: *Not exactly. I think you paint because you love to paint. I just think that sometimes, especially when you are mad at me for something, you paint so you won't have to deal with me.*

Jennifer: *So you are saying sometimes I use painting as a way to avoid you. Is that right?*

Andrew: *Yes. Sometimes you do.*

Jennifer: *Okay. Thank you for mentioning that. I imagine it feels like that sometimes.*

Andrew: *Another Exit you didn't mention is being too tired on Friday nights to make love.*

(And so on.)

EXERCISE

Closing My Exits

Suggested time: 20 minutes.

STEP 1.
On pages 108 and 109, working individually with your own list of Exits (including your partner's additions), place a check mark in column 1 next to the Exits you are willing to eliminate or reduce at the present time.

STEP 2.
In column 3, place an X next to the behaviors that would be difficult for you to change.

STEP 3.
Pick at least one of the Exits you identified in Step 1 that you realistically feel you can close or reduce beginning now.

STEP 4.
On the agreement form on page 116, fill in this week's date in the appropriate space.

STEP 5.
Make an agreement to close or reduce the Exit(s) you identified in Step 3. Complete the sentence, *"Specifically,* I agree to . . ." using positive language that says what you *will* do rather than what you *won't* do.

For example, if you agree to stop staying up late to surf the Web, you might write: "I agree to complete my work on the computer by eight each evening so that we can spend more time together. I will also help you more with the children."

If your Exit is creating large projects in the garden to keep you busy and away from your partner, you might write: "I agree to talk with you about the garden and invite you to work with me so we can have a shared activity."

- If you are clear about what you *will* do, rather than only what you *won't* do, you will find it much easier to change your behavior.
- Closing your Exits is a gradual process. In order for it to be effective, take it one step at a time. Give yourself a chance to integrate one or two new behaviors, before adding others.
- If you are contemplating leaving your relationship through any of the four Catastrophic Exits—suicide, murder, insanity, or divorce—include them in this initial

"Agreement to Close Exits," no matter how difficult you feel it will be, at least through the completion of *The New Couples' Study Guide* process. And we strongly encourage you to find an Imago therapist. Go to www.ImagoRelationships.com or call 1-800-729-1121.

STEP 6.
Sign your Agreement.

STEP 7.
When you have completed your Agreements, read them aloud to each other.

STEP 8.
Thank your partner for being willing to close or reduce the use of these Exits.

AGREEMENT TO CLOSE EXITS

Starting this week, _____ (date), I agree to

reserve more time and energy for our relationship. Specifically, I agree to

Signed, _____

STEP 9.
Read the Points to Remember together now.

STEP 10.
Answer the Review Questions together, noting your answers in the spaces provided.

STEP 11.
Read the Between-Session Assignments together now.

STEP 12.
If you have not scheduled a regular time for your sessions, make an appointment for your next session now. (Note: Session 7 is two hours long.)

POINTS TO REMEMBER

- An Exit is any behavior that allows us to reduce or avoid involvement in our relationships. We can use activities such as napping or volunteering at church as Exits. These activities, in themselves, are not necessarily Exits, but we are using them, at least in part, to avoid dealing with our partners.

- When we avoid our partners, we are avoiding ourselves. We are placing ourselves in conflict with our own inner agenda to heal our Childhood Wounds.

- We cannot change a habit simply by eliminating the old habit; we must have a very specific, new habit to substitute for it.

REVIEW QUESTIONS

Why might you feel increased tension and discomfort as you begin Closing Exits?

What are the benefits of Closing the Exits to your relationship?

BETWEEN-SESSION ASSIGNMENTS

1. **Close the Exit(s) you agreed to close or reduce.**
2. **Review Chapter 8, "Creating a Zone of Safety" in** *Getting the Love You Want* **before Session 7.**
3. **Continue:**
   - One day this week, record three things that your partner does that please you, and share those three things with him or her at the end of the day. Continue using the form for this in the Appendix on pages 240–242 and keeping track of the date in column 1.
   - Visualize your partner as a wounded child, especially in conflict situations and when he or she behaves in ways that frustrate you.
   - Use the Couple's Dialogue as a habitual part of your communication with your partner, especially in times of conflict.
   - Read your Mutual Relationship Vision together at least once before Session 7.

Re-Romanticizing Your Relationship I: Caring Behaviors

REVIEW in *Getting the Love You Want*
Chapter 8, "Creating a Zone of Safety."

TIME FRAME:
2 hours.

OBJECTIVES

• Create an emotional safety zone for you and your partner.

• Clearly identify the behaviors that make you feel loved and cared for.

• Know exactly what behaviors make your partner feel loved and cared for.

• Increase your feelings of pleasure with your partner.

• Restore conflict-free, caring interactions of romantic love.

THEORY

In the early, romantic stage of our relationships, we freely exchanged behaviors with our partners that were pleasurable. Although we may not have thought of it at the time, those pleasurable exchanges were intuitive responses to each other's childhood needs. We gave those caring behaviors gratefully in exchange for the promise of having our dreams fulfilled. As time passed and it appeared our romantic illusion of dream fulfillment was not going to happen, we discontinued those behaviors, or we began to keep score, measuring out a certain amount of this for a certain amount of that.

Those intuitively given caring behaviors touched our Childhood Wounds; they answered our unmet childhood needs. If we wish to create a Conscious Marriage, we must intentionally restore those loving exchanges by Re-Romanticizing our relationships.

Re-Romanticizing a relationship has three parts: Caring Behaviors, surprises, and high-energy Fun. We will focus on Caring Behaviors in this session and on surprises and fun in Session 8.

Caring Behaviors are easily given, conflict-free ways of showing our love for each other. They are target-specific behaviors, meaning they are specific behaviors that we have learned make *our partners* feel loved and cared for, not necessarily the same behaviors that make *us* feel loved and cared for. Most important, Caring Behaviors are *gifts*. They come without a price tag. They are not bartering tools; they are an opportunity to give pleasure to our partners. Our need to receive gifts comes straight out of childhood. We need to be loved and care for *unconditionally,* without having to do anything in return.

In order to speak our partners' language of love with behaviors that are specifically effective for them, we need to know what those behaviors are. We all expect our partners to know instinctively what we want, and we are angry when they don't decipher our unspoken needs. In a Conscious Marriage, we give our partners information about how they can touch our heart. We have erroneously believed that our partners (just as our parents were supposed to) always know exactly what we want without being told. Our childish unwillingness and our lack of practice at being specific about what we want and asking for it, coupled with our belief that our partners can read our minds, force us to play a guessing game: "Is this what you want? Is this?" It is time to learn to ask for exactly what we want. If we withhold that information or assume that our partners know it without being asked, we deprive them of the ability to express love to us effectively.

Reinstating daily Caring Behaviors will quickly restore a sense of love and goodwill to your relationship and will help to establish a zone of emotional safety between you and your partner. Emotional safety is a prerequisite for intimacy. When you treat each other the way you did in happier times, you begin to identify each other as a source of pleasure once again. Daily repetitions of positive behaviors cause your old brain to perceive your partner as "someone who nurtures me" rather than "bringer of death." Giving a prescribed number of Caring Behaviors a day regardless of the behaviors your partner gives you and regardless of how you are feeling toward your partner at the moment defeats the tit-for-tat mentality of the power struggle. You are no longer irrevocably at war. You can put your energy into healing your issues instead of defending against each other or blaming each other for causing or exacerbating your pain. As you Re-Romanticize your relationship, not only do you improve your immediate relationship, but you also begin to heal old wounds by giving each other the love you really want.

EXERCISE

Caring Behaviors

Suggested time: 1 hour and 15 minutes.

STEP 1.

On pages 125 and 126 in column 3, write everything your partner is already doing that makes you feel loved and cared about.

- You are completing the sentence "I feel loved and cared about when you . . ."
- Be specific, and phrase your statements positively.
  Write: "Introduce me to people at parties."
  Rather than: "Don't ignore me at parties."

STEP 2.

On the next worksheet, on pages 127 and 128 in column 3, write all the things your partner used to do in the romantic phase of your relationship that made you feel loved and cared about and that he or she is no longer doing.

- You are completing the sentence "I used to feel loved and cared about when you . . ."
- Again, be specific, and phrase your sentences positively.

STEP 3.

Moving to the next worksheet on pages 129 and 130 in column 3, write all the loving, caring behaviors you have always wanted but have never asked for.

- You are completing the sentence "I would feel loved and cared about if you . . ."
- These behaviors may come from experience or from your vision of a perfect mate. They may be private fantasies or secret desires.
- Quantify your requests. Be specific about how much and how often. For example: "Massage me for thirty minutes without stopping." "Go backpacking with me three times each summer." "Read a novel to me during Christmas vacation."
- Some of your responses to earlier exercises may be relevant:
  - "My Deepest Unfulfilled Desires" (page 61, Session 3).
  - "What I want most from my partner and don't get or don't get enough of" (page 87, Partner Profile, Session 5).
  - "Behaviors I Would Like from My Partner" (page 95, Session 5).

STEP 4.

In column 2 on the three worksheets, indicate how important each Caring Behavior is to you on a scale of 1 to 5.

- A 1 indicates "very important," and a 5 indicates "not so important."

STEP 5.

Exchange study guides with your partner. Read your partner's completed list of Caring Behaviors, and put an X in column 1 next to any behaviors you are not willing to do at this time.

- The behaviors you and your partner feel you cannot do now will be addressed in a later session.

STEP 6.

From your partner's list, pick at least one Caring Behavior that she or he has marked with a 1, to give to her or him today. Pick a behavior that is easy for you to give.

- When you have chosen a Caring Behavior to give to your partner, return his or her study guide to him or her.

STEP 7.

Add to your list of Caring Behaviors (pages 125–130) at any time.

- Tell your partner when you update your list.
- Indicate the importance (with a number from 1 to 5 in column 2) of each additional Caring Behavior.
- Your partner may X your additions if they are too difficult to give at the moment.

STEP 8.

Whenever your partner gives you one of your requested Caring Behaviors, acknowledge it appreciatively.

CARING BEHAVIORS

1 Not at this time X	2 Importance 1–5	3 I feel loved and cared about when you . . .

1 Not at this time X	2 Importance 1–5	3 I feel loved and cared about when you . . .

CARING BEHAVIORS

1 Not at this time X	2 Importance 1–5	3 I *used to* feel loved and cared about when you . . .

1 Not at this time X	2 Importance 1–5	3 I *used to* feel loved and cared about when you . . .

CARING BEHAVIORS

1 Not at this time X	2 Importance 1–5	3 I *would* feel loved and cared about if you . . .

1 Not at this time X	2 Importance 1–5	3 I *would* feel loved and cared about if you . . .

EXERCISE

Continuing to Close Exits

Suggested time: 30 minutes.

△   Since this is a short session, you can spend 30 minutes with your partner now continuing the process of Closing Exits that you began in Session 6. You can do the same at the end of the next session as well. Thereafter, continuing to Close Exits will become a part of your ongoing Between-Session Assignments.

STEP 1.
Acknowledge your partner for the Exits he or she has already closed or reduced.

STEP 2.
Have a Couple's Dialogue for 15 minutes about your feelings and thoughts about closing or reducing exits.

- Include
  ~your feelings about the Exits you have closed or reduced,
  ~the effect of closing or reducing these Exits, and
  ~any more Exits you or your partner have identified for yourselves or each other.

STEP 3.
If your partner identifies any additional Exits for you, use the modified Couple's Dialogue from Steps 5 and 6 on page 110 to clarify them.

- Use Mirroring to clarify your understanding of each additional Exit that your partner feels you use.
- End each Mirroring transaction with a Validation.
- For example: "Thank you," or "I can see how that might feel like an Exit to you."

STEP 4.
Include any additional Exits identified by you or your partner on your list on pages 108 and 109.

- Add every Exit your partner feels you use, whether you agree with it or not.

STEP 5.

Look over your list on pages 108 and 109 and choose at least one more Exit to close or reduce.

STEP 6.

In the Appendix on pages 243–248, fill out another "Agreement to Close Exits" form.

- Write this week's date in the appropriate space.
- Complete the sentence, "Specifically I agree to . . ." using positive language that says what you *will* do rather than what you *won't* do.
- Sign your Agreement.
- When you have completed your Agreements, read them aloud to each other.
- Thank your partner for being willing to close or reduce the use of these Exits.

STEP 7.

Read the Points to Remember together now.

STEP 8.

Answer the Review Questions together, noting your answers in the spaces provided.

STEP 9.

Read the Between-Session Assignments together now.

STEP 10.

If you have not scheduled a regular time for your sessions, make an appointment for your next session now. (Note Session 8 is 1 hour and 30 minutes long.)

POINTS TO REMEMBER

- The exchange of pleasurable behaviors creates a zone of emotional safety for you and your partner. Emotional safety is a prerequisite for intimacy.

- Caring Behaviors are gifts. They are not demands or bargains. There is no obligation to reciprocate.

- Caring Behaviors are target-specific behaviors, guided by the information your partner has provided about exactly how to touch his or her heart.

- Giving daily Caring Behaviors helps you and your partner to perceive each other as nurturing rather than hurtful and allows you to focus on healing your wounds rather than defending them from each other.

- Giving you partner information about how he or she can touch your heart allows him or her to express love to you effectively.

REVIEW QUESTIONS

Why is it valuable to give your partner daily Caring Behaviors regardless of the number of Caring Behaviors he or she gives you?

Why is it important to create a zone of emotional safety?

How will the giving of Caring Behaviors affect the power struggle in your relationship?

BETWEEN-SESSION ASSIGNMENTS

1. **In the next day or two, transfer your partner's list of Caring Behaviors to your own study guide, on the worksheet in the Appendix. Transfer the number indicating the importance of the behavior to your partner as well.**

2. **Give your partner at least one Caring Behavior every day this week.**
   - Give them regardless of how you feel about your partner and regardless of the number of Caring Behaviors your partner gives you.
   - The principle behind making behavioral changes is that if we act differently, we will feel differently. Even if you experience resistance to this exercise, keep giving the Caring Behaviors anyway. Over time, your feelings will change.

3. **Acknowledge appreciatively every Caring Behavior your partner gives you.**

4. **Add to your list of Caring Behaviors as new ones occur to you. Tell your partner you are making an addition, and allow him or her to write the new behavior in his or her study guide as well.**

5. **Review "The Surprise List" and "The Fun List" sections of Chapter 8 in *Getting the Love You Want* before Session 8.**

6. **Continue:**
   - Close or reduce the Exit(s) you have agreed upon.
   - One day this week, write down three things that your partner does that please you, and share those three things with him or her at the end of the day. Continue using the agreements in the Appendix, keeping track of the date in column 1.
   - Visualize your partner as a wounded child, especially in conflict situations and when he or she behaves in ways that frustrate you.
   - Use the Couple's Dialogue as a habitual part of your communication with your partner, especially in times of conflict.
   - Read your Mutual Relationship Vision together at least once before Session 8.

Re-Romanticizing Your Relationship II: Surprises and Fun

REVIEW in *Getting the Love You Want*
"The Surprise List" and "The Fun List" in Chapter 8.

TIME FRAME:
1 hour and 30 minutes.

OBJECTIVES

- Restore or deepen the passion in your relationship.

- Intensify the emotional bond between you and your partner.

THEORY
Pleasurable stimulus loses a part of its effectiveness if it is repeated with predictable regularity. Oddly enough, for all our fear of change and the unknown, human beings need a certain amount of random, unexpected input of new experiences. We require both comfort and excitement to feel fully alive. Augmenting the pleasurable comfort of receiving daily Caring Behaviors with the excitement generated by receiving unpredictable surprises and having exuberant fun with each other effectively reintroduces the passion of early romance back into our relationships.

Surprises are random rather than regularly occurring Caring Behaviors. Because of the way our neural system works, Caring Behaviors lose their intensity over time; we have a way of normalizing any stimulus that is repeated often. To maintain a high level of pleasure in our relationships, we need to begin giving our partners surprises—unexpected Caring Behaviors at unpredictable times. We get to be detectives, listening carefully to our partners' offhanded comments:

- "My grandmother bakes the best oatmeal cookies."
- "I haven't seen a Bugs Bunny cartoon in years."
- "Boy, don't these pictures of rafting down the Colorado River look great?"
- "I'd love to go to a circus again someday."
- "I used to love the violets that grew in our yard."

These comments provide clues to their secret wishes and dreams. Surprises, like Caring Behaviors, are target-specific gifts. We give our partners what they want rather than what would please us, or what we think would please them. We operate in their frame of reference rather than our own.

Fun is a high-energy or intense activity that produces deep pleasure and/or laughter. In the final analysis, Fun may be our most important activity. A direct correlation exists between our feelings of pleasure and our sense of safety with our partners. Pleasure brings enlivement—the awakening or reawakening of our life force, our aliveness. Our old brain equates pleasure with aliveness and therefore with survival and safety. The more pleasure we give each other, the more safety we feel together, the deeper our bond, and the more spontaneous the exchange of Fun Behaviors, because our old brain relaxes in an environment it perceives to be safe. Examples of Fun activities include telling jokes, chasing each other, dancing to compelling music, spinning like whirling dervishes, massage, and sex. More passive activities, such as watching TV or reading together, probably will not produce this exuberant, energizing effect. Competitive activities, such as tennis or golf, may not achieve the desired exuberantly pleasurable effect, either. Competitive activities qualify as Fun only if we can engage in the activity without stirring up tension.

If your relationship is conflicted, you may have difficulty having Fun together. You may also have some resistance to Fun because of an absence in our society of an adult model for playing together or because of prohibitions carried over from your childhood. Many parents inhibit high-energy play because it is such a strong expression of basic life energy that it frightens them. You may have unconsciously picked up this attitude. If so, consciously go against it, and experiment with letting go of those old prohibitions. Remember, the principle behind behavioral change is that if we act differently, we will feel differently. When a child, for example, asks you to play ball or race him or her up the block, you may not feel like it, but if you do it wholeheartedly anyway, your feelings begin to shift, and you find yourself having Fun. You can *do* Fun activities in order to generate feelings of Fun; you don't have to be magically struck with feeling Fun first.

Re-Romanticizing your relationship with the comfort of Caring Behaviors and the excitement of unpredictable Surprises and exuberant Fun will increase your associations of pleasure with your partner, which in turn will increase your feelings of safety and open the door to deeply satisfying, joyous intimacy between you.

EXERCISE

Surprises for My Partner

Suggested time: 15 minutes.

Δ   Do this exercise individually, and keep it secret from your partner.

STEP 1.
On the worksheet on pages 139 and 141 in column 2, make a list of things you could do for your partner that would be especially pleasing to him or her if received from you unexpectedly.

- Create your list from memories of things that have pleased your partner in the past and from hints and offhanded comments your partner has made.
- Do not guess. This is a list of target-specific Surprises, things you know would please your partner, not things you think he or she wants.
- Keep this list hidden from your partner at all times.

STEP 2.
Choose one item from your list to surprise your partner with this week.

STEP 3.
When you give the Surprise you have chosen, record the date in column 1.

- Recording the dates you give Surprises will help you keep track of what you have done and when. Try not to fall into a predictable partner. For example, Surprises given every Saturday soon become routine and even expected.

STEP 4.
Add to your list of Surprises for your partner continually.

- This is an ongoing process. Think of yourself as a detective ferreting out your partner's hidden wishes and desires. Listen carefully to him or her for clues.

STEP 5.
When you receive a Surprise from your partner, acknowledge it appreciatively, and record the Surprise and the date you receive it on the worksheet on pages 143 and 145.

SURPRISES FOR MY PARTNER

1 Date	2 Surprises

1 Date	2 Surprises

SURPRISES RECEIVED FROM MY PARTNER

1 Date	2 Surprises received

1 Date	2 Surprises received

EXERCISE

Fun

Suggested Time: 30 minutes.

STEP 1.

On the worksheet on page 148, make a list of exciting, high-energy, Fun activities you would like to do with your partner.

- Fun is behavior that needs no skill, has no rules, can't be done wrong, causes a belly laugh, and can produce a beneficial, energizing effect in just a few minutes. For example: "belly laughing," "dancing," "wrestling," "showers together," "sex," "massage," "jumping up and down," "jumping rope," "chasing each other," "water fighting."
- Include face-to-face experiences that are physically vigorous and emotionally intense.
- Include activities that involve pleasurable body contact.
- Include ways you remember having Fun with other children when you were a child.
- Include ways you had Fun with your partner when you were in the romantic phase of your relationship.
- Use your imagination, and make up ways to have Fun with your partner.

STEP 2.

One at a time, read your list of Fun activities aloud to each other.

STEP 3.

On pages 149 and 150 in your study guides, make a mutual list of fun activities that combines all of your ideas.

STEP 4.

With your partner, pick one activity on your combined list to do today.

- If it is an activity that you need to schedule time for, do so now.
- You may experience some resistance to taking part in such exuberant, childlike activities, especially if you are in conflict with your partner. Do this exercise anyway. Allow doing something Fun with your partner to generate feelings of Fun between you. Keep doing Fun activities together until having Fun begins to feel familiar and, therefore, safe.

STEP 5.

Pick a Fun item from your partner's list that would stretch you into a new experience.

- Invite your partner to lead you through it.
- Be aware of your resistance, and challenge any fears you may have, but also listen to any voice in your head that warns you about the danger of this way of having Fun.

MY FUN LIST

OUR FUN LIST

OUR FUN LIST

EXERCISE

Continuing to Close Exits

Suggested time: 30 minutes.

△   Since this is a short session, you can spend 30 minutes with your partner now continuing the process of Closing Exits that you began in Session 6. Hereafter, continuing to Close Exits will become a part of your ongoing Between-Session Assignments.

STEP 1.
Acknowledge your partner for the Exits he or she has already closed or reduced.

STEP 2.
Have a Couple's Dialogue with your partner about your feelings and thoughts regarding the Exits you have closed or reduced and any more Exits you have identified for yourselves or each other.

STEP 3.
If your partner identifies any additional Exits for you, use the modified Couple's Dialogue from Steps 5 and 6 in "Identifying My Partner's Exits" (page 110, Session 6) to clarify them, using Mirroring to clarify each Exit and ending each Mirroring transaction with a Validation.

STEP 4.
Include any additional Exits identified by you or your partner on your list. Add every Exit your partner feels you use, whether you agree with it or not.

STEP 5.
Choose at least one more Exit from your list to close or reduce.

STEP 6.
Fill out another "Agreement to Close Exits" form in the Appendix on pages 243–248. Sign it, and read it aloud to your partner.

STEP 7.
Thank your partner for being willing to Close or Reduce the Exits he or she has chosen.

STEP 8.
Read the Points to Remember together now.

STEP 9.

Answer the Review Questions together, noting your answers in the spaces provided.

STEP 10.

Read the Between-Session Assignments together now.

STEP 11.

If you have not scheduled a regular time for your sessions, make an appointment for your next session now. (Note: Session 9 is very full and may take up to 2 hours and 30 minutes.)

POINTS TO REMEMBER

- The principle behind behavioral change is that if we act differently, we will feel differently. Doing appropriate activities can generate a desired feeling, rather than waiting to be magically struck with the feeling first.

- We require both comfort and excitement to feel fully alive and satisfied.

- There is a direct correlation between our feelings of pleasure and our sense of safety with our partners; the more pleasure, the more safety. Our old brains equate pleasure with aliveness and survival.

REVIEW QUESTIONS

Why is it valuable to give Surprises and have Fun with your partner even if you don't feel like it?

How does giving Surprises Re-Romanticize your relationship?

Why is exuberant, childlike Fun so important to your relationship?

BETWEEN-SESSION ASSIGNMENTS

1. Remove your "Surprises for My Partner" list from your study guide, and keep it hidden from your partner at all times.

2. Give your partner the Surprise you chose at some unexpected time this week.
   - Enjoy your partner's response when you give him or her the Surprise.
   - As you identify more of your partner's secret wishes and desires, add them to your Surprise list.
   - Record the date you give the Surprise.

3. When you receive a Surprise from your partner, thank him or her. Record the Surprises you receive from your partner, including the date you receive them.

4. Do at least one high-energy Fun activity with your partner each day this week.
   - Just a minute or two of a high-energy activity will be enlivening.
   - Even if you experience resistance to taking part in such exuberant, childlike activities, do this exercise anyway. Allow *doing* something Fun with your partner to generate *feelings* of fun between you.

5. Review Chapter 10, "Defining Your Curriculum," in *Getting the Love You Want* before Session 9.

6. Continue:
   - Get together with your partner for 20 minutes before Session 9 to have a Couple's Dialogue about the Exits you have closed and reduced and to choose at least one more Exit to close or reduce.
     - Acknowledge your partner for the Exits he or she has closed or reduced.
     - Use the modified Couple's Dialogue (with mirroring and a simple validation) to clarify any additional Exits your partner identifies for you.
     - Include any additional Exits on your list on pages 108 and 109.
     - Choose at least one more Exit to close or reduce next. Fill out another "Agreement to Close" Exits form (Appendix), and read it aloud to your partner.
     - Thank your partner for being willing to close or reduce the Exit he or she has chosen.
   - Close or reduce the Exit(s) you have agreed upon.
   - Give your partner at least one Caring Behavior every day this week. Continue to add to your list on pages 125–130 as new behaviors

occur to you. Acknowledge appreciatively every Caring Behavior your partner gives you.

- One day this week, write down three things that your partner does that please you (separate from Caring Behaviors, Surprises, and Fun) and share them with him or her at the end of the day. Use pages 249–251 in the Appendix. Include the date in column 1.
- Visualize your partner as a wounded child, especially in conflict situations and when he or she behaves in ways that frustrate you.
- Use the Couple's Dialogue as a habitual part of your communication with your partner, especially in times of conflict.
- Read your Mutual Relationship Vision together at least once before Session 9.

RESTRUCTURING
FRUSTRATIONS

REVIEW in *Getting the Love You Want*
Chapter 10, "Defining Your Curriculum."

TIME FRAME:
Up to 2 hours and 30 minutes. This is a very full session, and may take longer than 2 hours. (See Between-Session Assignment 1, page 173.)

OBJECTIVES

- Educate each other about your deepest needs.
- Replace criticisms and complaints about your partner with positively expressed requests for behavior changes.
- Heal your partner by changing to meeting his or her deepest needs.
- Recover your essential wholeness by Stretching to meet your partner's deepest needs.

THEORY
As we Re-Romanticize our relationships we re-identify our partners as the people who are going to make us whole. And we discover once again that what we want most from our partners is what they are most unable to give. The environmental safety that Re-Romanticizing creates, however, enables us to address these deeper unresolved issues.

The skills required for healing our deepest wounds are the same skills we have been practicing in the less conflicted arenas of Re-Romanticizing our relationships. We have been telling our partners exactly what we want, and we have been gifting our partners with what they have asked for. In order to address our deepest wounds, we apply these same actions to the more highly conflicted areas of our relationships. Even as we are now addressing more complex challenges, we continue to practice the principle of graduated change, making the changes that are easiest to make first.

As we know, the agenda of our old brains is to get our original caretakers to change to meet our needs or to get someone so like those who originally wounded us that our old brains can't tell the difference to change to meet our needs. In other words, to heal our Childhood Wounds, our perfect Imago partners must change and give us what we need. Our partners, of course, have this same agenda with us.

The Stretching exercise presented in this session is based on the premise that we are perfectly matched with someone who needs *us* to change *exactly as we* need to in order to heal *their* wounds and recover *our own* wholeness. It is obvious how our partners benefit if we meet their needs. They get what they want. However, it is less obvious to us how we benefit from making such fundamental changes in ourselves. Let's look first at what the Stretching exercise is and, second, at how it works to help us recover *our own* wholeness.

On the giving end, Stretching involves overcoming discomfort and resistance to give our partners what they need to heal their Childhood Wounds. Since what our partners need is often what is most difficult for us to give, we are called upon to overcome—to Stretch—in order to meet our partners' requests.

On the receiving or requesting end, Stretching involves identifying the unmet childhood needs behind our chronic Frustrations with our partners. We express these needs positively, as Desires to be satisfied. For example, if your Frustration is "You always withdraw when I am upset," your Desire might be "I would like you to comfort me when I'm upset." If your Frustration is "I don't like it when you tell me my opinion is stupid," your Desire might be "I would like you to value my different perspective." We then translate these general Desires into specific requests for behavior changes.

A Behavior Change Request is a positively phrased, very specific, measurable, doable behavior that we would like from our partners instead of the behavior we find so frustrating. We make sure that our partners have all the information they need to give us what we want with no room for guessing or misinterpretation. And, again, these behavior changes are *gifts*. Giving our partners information about what we want or need in no way obligates our partners to do what we ask. When we do Stretch to meet our partners' needs by granting a Behavior Change Request, we do so with no strings attached.

We can probably see how Stretching to meet our needs would make our partners healthier and more whole. It is easier to understand the value in making such fundamental changes when we look at someone else. Let's now examine the following examples to begin to understand how Stretching to meet your *partner's* needs will make *you* more healthy:

> Allen, as an only child, felt suffocated by his mother's constant focus of attention on him. Marni, his partner, grew up in a very large family where all of life was a group activity. Allen needs much more space and time to himself than Marni is willing to give him. If Marni were able to give Allen the time alone and space he needs, not only would she be helping Allen heal his wound around his suffocating mother, but she would also heal her unacknowledged fear of being alone and recover her own ability to enjoy having time and space to herself.
>
> In another example, Louise's father spent a lot of time away from the family working in order to support them. Louise has chosen a husband, Matthew, who often puts his work before his home life. Louise would like Matthew to give their relationship more priority in his life and spend more time with her. Meeting Louise's need for more time and energy from him triggers Matthew's fears of intimacy and of having enough time and energy to work hard enough to take care of himself in the world. If Matthew would spend more time with Louise, not only would Louise get the support and attention she craves, but Matthew would recover his denied need for closeness and would heal his fear that no one else will take care of him.

The truth is that both partners in an Imago relationship have identical needs, except that what is openly acknowledged in one is repressed or denied in the other or vice versa. When the partner with the denied need is able to Stretch and overcome his or her resistance and satisfy the other partner's acknowledged need, the old brain, which does not distinguish between other and self, interprets the Caring Behavior as inner-directed, and that partner *receives* the gift he or she has just given. For example, Marni has permission to experience her own forgotten joy in being alone, and Matthew can feel close to and supported in the world by another person.

Resistance to the Stretching exercise may surface in two ways. More obviously, we may feel resistance to making changes in ourselves, for in doing so we are breaking down long-standing defenses and awakening traits we were told were unacceptable. (Remember, the greater our resistance to a particular change, the greater potential for growth that change contains.) Less obviously, resistance may come up around actually having our deepest Desires satisfied. Underneath every wish is a fear of having that wish come true. When our partners start treating us the way we always wanted, we experience a strange combination of pleasure and fear. We like what our partners are doing, but a part of us feels that we don't deserve it and believes we are violating a powerful taboo in accepting such unaccustomed pleasure. We may find ways to undermine or sabotage the positive behavior. Resistance to the satisfaction of a deeply held need is more common than most of us might believe. The way to overcome our fear and resistance is to keep going courageously with the process of Stretching until our anxiety becomes more manageable. We learn by repetition. Given enough time, we learn that the taboos that have been impeding our growth are ghosts of the past and have no real power in our present-day lives.

A constant, committed practice of informing our partners of our needs and Stretching to meet their needs creates profound changes in our relationships. We feel better about ourselves because we are able to satisfy our partners' fundamental needs, which makes us more willing to keep Stretching beyond our resistance into even more positive and nurturing behaviors. There is a mutual healing. The partner who requested the behavior change experiences unresolved childhood needs being met; the partner who makes the changes recovers essential parts of her or his being and satisfies repressed or denied needs that he or she was unaware of having. The deeper our commitment to creating a Conscious Marriage and the deeper our understanding that Stretching to heal our partner heals us as well, the more willing we can be to give the gift of a requested behavioral change.

The Stretching exercise is an essential skill in a positive working relationship. When it becomes your standard method for dealing with criticism and conflict, you will have reached a new stage in your journey toward a conscious marriage. You will have moved beyond the Power Struggle, beyond the stage of awakening, into the stage of transformation.

EXERCISE

Stretching

Suggested time: 1 hour and 45 minutes.

STEP 1.

On the worksheet on pages 164–165 in column 1, make a comprehensive list of all your chronic Frustrations with your partner.

- Transfer all your Frustrations from the "Frustrations with My Partner" worksheet in Session 5, pages 90–91.
- Add any more chronic criticisms or complaints about your partner to your list.
- Phrase your Frustrations as if you were completing the sentence, "I don't like it when . . ."

For example: "You drive too fast."

"You are always late."

- There is a sample of this exercise following the worksheet on page 168. Note: All examples describe behaviors. They omit feelings, thoughts, and traits. You can ask only for behavior changes, not changes inside your partner such as feelings, thoughts, and traits.

STEP 2.

Identify the Desire (the deep, unmet need) that lies hidden behind each Frustration, and write these Desires in column 2.

For example: Frustration: "I don't like it when you drive too fast."

Desire: "I would like to feel safe and relaxed when you are driving."

Frustration: "I don't like it when you're always late."

Desire: "I want you to be more reliable about time."

Frustration: "I don't like it when I always have to initiate making love."

Desire: "I want to feel as if you desire me."

- Refer to the sample exercise following the worksheet.
- Phrase each of your Desires positively. Write what you *do* want rather than what you *don't* want.

Write: "I would like to feel safe and relaxed when you are driving."

Rather than: "I don't want to feel scared when you drive."

- Think of each Desire as an unmet need. Go beyond, "I want you to drive more slowly." Why do you want your partner to drive more slowly? What deep need of yours is asking to be met?
- You may want to refer to the Session 5 worksheets to help you identify your Desires—the deep unmet needs behind your Frustrations.

STEP 3.

On the next worksheet on pages 166–167 in column 1, copy the first Desire from your list on the first worksheet.

STEP 4.

In column 4, describe positively expressed, very specific ways your partner can help satisfy that Desire.

For example:

Desire:	"I want you to be more reliable about time."
Behavior Change Request:	"When you are going to be more than 15 minutes late for any appointment or date we make, I would like you to call me as soon as you know."

- After the worksheet there is a completed sample of this exercise on page 168.
- Whenever possible, quantify your requests. How much? For how long? How many? Exactly when?
- You may think of several specific Behavior Change Requests for one Desire. Record them all.
- Write each request on its own line.
- Again, write what you *do* want rather than what you *don't* want.

STEP 5.

Repeat Steps 3 and 4 until you have translated all of your Desires into specific Behavior Change Requests.

- At the end of your list, add any of your Caring Behaviors (from pages 125–130) that your partner had marked with an X.

STEP 6.
Share pages 164–167 of your worksheets with your partner, either by exchanging lists and reading to yourselves or reading your lists aloud to each other.

STEP 7.
Use Mirroring and a simple Validation to clarify any Desires or Behavior Change Requests you do not understand.

- Rewrite any requests, if necessary, until each behavior is so clearly described that your partner knows exactly what you want.

STEP 8.
In column 3, on the worksheet, indicate how important each Behavior Change Request is to you on a scale of 1 to 5.

- A 1 indicates "very important," and a 5 indicates "not so important."
- Rank each individual request, even when several of them apply to the same Desire.

STEP 9.
Exchange Study Guides with your partner. On your partner's list in column 5, use the numbers 1 to 5 to indicate how difficult each behavior change would be for you to make.

- A 1 indicates "very difficult," and a 5 indicates "easy."

STEP 10.
Pick the request that is easiest for you, and grant it this week.

- These behavior changes are gifts. Grant them regardless of how you feel about your partner and regardless of how many changes your partner is making.
- You are under no obligation to make any specific changes, but remember that each change you make will help you become whole and will help heal your partner's wounds.
- You may feel a lot of resistance to responding to your partner's needs in this way, because these behaviors are not familiar and comfortable to you. Remember, the more difficult a particular exercise seems to you, the more potential it contains for growth.

- This exercise is very difficult and very important to the creation of your Conscious Marriage.
- You will continue, over time, to grant your partner at least one Behavior Change Request per week until you have granted them all.

STEP 11.

Continue to translate Frustrations into Desires and then into specific Behavior Change Requests. Add new Desires and Requests to your list as they occur to you.

- In column 3, indicate the importance of each new request you add.
- Be sure to share any new Desires and Requests with your partner.

STEP 12.

When your partner Stretches and grants one of your Behavior Change Requests, acknowledge him or her appreciatively.

STRETCHING

1 Frustration I don't like it when . . .	2 Desire	3 Importance to me 1–5 (very important to not so important)	4 Behavior Change Request	5 Difficulty for my partner 1–5 (very difficult to easy)

1 Frustration I don't like it when . . .	2 Desire	3 Importance to me 1–5 (very important to not so important)	4 Behavior Change Request	5 Difficulty for my partner 1–5 (very difficult to easy)

STRETCHING

1 Frustration I don't like it when . . .	2 Desire	3 Importance to me 1–5 (very important to not so important)	4 Behavior Change Request	5 Difficulty for my partner 1–5 (very difficult to easy)

1 Frustration I don't like it when . . .	2 Desire	3 Importance to me 1–5 (very important to not so important)	4 Behavior Change Request	5 Difficulty for my partner 1–5 (very difficult to easy)

STRETCHING
sample

1 Frustration I don't like it when . . .	2 Desire	3 Importance to me 1–5 (very important to not so important)	4 Behavior Change Request	5 Difficulty for my partner 1–5 (very difficult to easy)
You are always late.	I want you to be more reliable about time.	1	When you are going to be more than 15 minutes late for any appointment or date that we make, I would like you to call me as soon as you know.	3
		2	If you are going to be more than ½ hour late coming home from work, please call me by 5:30.	3
		1	When we go out, start getting ready ½ hour before we leave so we can leave on time.	4
		1	When we go to the movies, be ready to leave in time to get to the theatre 15 minutes early so that we can see the previews.	5
You drive too fast.	I want to feel safe and relaxed when you drive.	3	When you are driving, I would like you to obey the speed limit.	4
		1	If the road conditions are bad, I would like you to drive even more slowly.	5
I always have to initiate making love.	I want to feel like you desire me.	1	I would like you to initiate making love at least twice a week.	1
You are always tired and distant when you come home from work.	I would like to feel that you are happy to see me.	2	I would like you to give me a warm hug as soon as you come home.	4
You withdraw when I'm upset or crying.	I would like you to comfort me when I'm upset.	1	When I tell you that I'm upset, I would like you to put your arms around me and give me your full attention.	3
You tell me my opinion is stupid.	I would like you to value my perspective.	1	When you ask my opinion, I would like you to listen fully to my response without interrupting and ask me a few questions, like an interviewer, to help me express my thoughts even more fully.	2
		2	I would like to have a Couple's Dialogue with you when you don't agree with my opinion, where you are the Receiver and I am the Sender.	4

EXERCISE

Translating a Frustration into a Behavior Change Request
Suggested Time: 10 minutes.

△   If you do not have time to do this exercise during your session, do it as a Between-Session Assignment.

△   This exercise is meant to help you verbally translate the Desire behind your impulse to criticize or complain about your partner into a positive Behavior Change Request. With a little practice, you will be able to do this instinctually when you get frustrated with your partner.

STEP 1.
Pick one of your Frustrations with your partner.

STEP 2.
On the top of the following worksheet on page 170, translate the Frustration into a positive Behavior Change Request by filling in the blanks with the appropriate information.

- The letter, page number, and/or description in parentheses refer to the location of the information to be used to complete the sentences.
- A completed sample translation appears before the worksheet.

STEP 3.
Practice directly translating your Frustrations into positive Behavior Change Requests by reading your completed sentences aloud to your partner.

- It will take a little practice to be able to make this direct translation spontaneously during a moment of frustration.
- There are two blank pages in the Appendix on pages 252 and 254 that you can use to practice as you are developing your ability to spontaneously and verbally make the translation from a Frustration into a positive Behavior Change Request.

TRANSLATING A FRUSTRATION INTO A BEHAVIOR CHANGE REQUEST
Sample

When you *ask me a question and then answer it yourself,* I feel *angry.* Then I react by *getting hard and opinionated,* to hide my fear of *being ignored.* I want *to feel heard and valued by you. When you ask me a question, please wait for me to fully answer it before you respond or state your opinion. I would like to tell you that I am finished before you start talking.*

When you (Frustrating Behavior, K): _____

_____

I feel (corresponding Feeling, L): _____

_____

Then I react by (corresponding Reaction, M): _____

_____

To hide my fear of (corresponding Fear, N): _____

_____

I want (corresponding Desire): _____

_____

(State the corresponding Behavior Change Request): _____

_____

_____

STEP 4.
Read the Points to Remember together now.

STEP 5.
Answer the Review Questions together, noting your answers in the spaces provided.

STEP 6.
Read the Between-Session Assignments together now.

STEP 7.
If you have not scheduled a regular time for your sessions, make an appointment for your next session now. (Note: Session 10 may take 2 hours and 30 minutes or longer.)

POINTS TO REMEMBER

- Behind every impulse to criticize or complain about our partners is a Desire for the satisfaction of an unmet childhood need.

- We are perfectly matched with someone who needs us to change exactly as we need to in order to heal their wounds and recover our own wholeness.

- Both partners in an IMAGO relationship have identical needs. What is openly acknowledged in one is repressed or denied in the other, and vice versa.

- Our level of resistance increases with the depth of the changes we are making. The greater our resistance to a particular change, the more potential for growth that change contains.

REVIEW QUESTIONS

How do we heal ourselves when we Stretch to meet our partners' needs?

What is the value of converting our Frustrations with our partners into Behavior Change Requests?

What is the difference between a Desire and a Behavior Change Request?

BETWEEN-SESSION ASSIGNMENTS

1. This is a very full session. If you do not complete all of the exercises in the time you have allotted for the session, make an appointment to complete them together as a Between-Session Assignment before Session 10.

2. Before Session 10, transfer your partner's Behavior Change Requests in *his* or *her* Study Guide to the Behavior Change Requests (pages 263–266) in the Appendix of *your* Study Guide. Transfer the numbers indicating the importance of these behavior changes to your partner as well.

   • When your partner thinks of new Behavior Change Requests, add them to your list on pages 263–266 in the Appendix of your study guide.

3. This week, grant your partner the easy Behavior Change Request you identified, noting the date it is granted next to the request on pages 263–266 in your study guide.

4. Translate your Frustrations with your partner directly into Behavior Change Requests whenever possible. The first few times, you can use pages 259–261 in the Appendix to help you process your Frustration.

   • All Behavior Change Requests are gifts, not obligations.

5. Review Chapter 11, "Containing Rage," in *Getting the Love You Want* before Session 10.

6. Continue:

   • Add to any of your lists as new thoughts occur to you. Inform your partner of additions to the lists that apply to him or her.

   • Do at least one high-energy Fun activity with your partner every day this week.

   • Give your partner another Surprise at an unexpected time this week, and enjoy his or her response. Be sure to record the date you gave the Surprise. Record Surprises received from your partner, with dates.

   • Give your partner at least one Caring Behavior every day this week.

   • Before Session 10, have a Couple's Dialogue with your partner about the Exits you have closed or reduced so far, and choose at least one more Exit to close or reduce.

   • Close or reduce the Exit(s) you have agreed upon.

   • One day this week, write down three things that your partner does that please you (separate from granted Behavior Change Requests, Caring Behaviors, Surprises, and Fun), and share them with him or her at the end of the day. Use the Appendix (pages 240–242), and include the date in column 1.

- Visualize your partner as a wounded child, especially in conflict situations and when he or she behaves in ways that frustrate you.
- Read your Mutual Relationship Vision together at least once before Session 10.

7. **Remember:**
- Give your partner the gifts of Caring Behaviors, Surprises, and granting Behavior Change Requests regardless of how you feel about your partner and regardless of how many gifts your partner gives you.
- Acknowledge your partner appreciatively for each gift he or she gives you—Behavior Change Requests, Surprises, Caring Behaviors, and any others.
- Engage in a high-energy Fun activity each day.
- Continue, even if you feel resistance to any of the exercises, to take the risk of doing something new and therefore perhaps uncomfortable, in order to create your Conscious Marriage. Remember, the more difficult a particular exercise seems to you, the more potential it contains for growth.

Resolving Your Rage

REVIEW in *Getting the Love You Want*
Chapter 11, "Containing Rage."

TIME FRAME:

2 hours and 30 minutes or longer. This is a full session and may take longer than 2 hours.

OBJECTIVES

- Create a safe and constructive environment in which to express intense feelings.

- Allow a safe reexperiencing of childhood rage, terror, and grief.

- Replace all disagreement and fighting with structured processes that allow rage to generate and sustain your aliveness, rather than threaten it.

- Regain your joyful aliveness by appropriately expressing rage and other intense feelings.

- Increase your capacity to feel and express love.

THEORY

The idea that we would be happier and healthier if we were fully in touch with our anger, fear, and pain goes against some powerful directives. We have been strongly conditioned by our parents and society to judge, repress, and deny these feelings, in particular our anger. We have been taught that anger is bad, destructive, and self-indulgent, and we should not feel it. Other intense feelings were also labeled unacceptable, and we learned not to show them. In childhood, our expressions of anger and sometimes even fear or pain, usually met with negative responses, such as punishment, being ignored, being yelled at, or being shamed. Our experience on the receiving end of anger or rage also probably verified what we had been taught about its destructive power.

Anger is like a fire. If we contain fire appropriately and allow it to burn safely, it nourishes us, keeps us alive, and provides us with warmth and light. If we let it rage out of control, it damages or destroys us. If we suffocate it and stamp it out, eventually the cold and the dark seep into our bones, and we become numb. Depression is a direct result of rage suppression. When we suppress our anger, the rest of our life force gets blocked as well. We suffocate our capacity to love. Appropriate expression of anger is the key to regaining the joyful aliveness that filled us as children. Releasing anger allows all of our other feelings to flow: fear, pain, sadness, joy, and love.

Feelings are our natural, appropriate, and necessary response to experience. We have been storing feelings since childhood. When our backed-up feelings are triggered by a current circumstance, we respond with out-of-proportion intensity. Just as we have our current partners fused with our early caretakers in order to heal our original wounds, a current stimulus often triggers our unexpressed childhood feelings so they can be processed and healed. In order for our rage and other suppressed feelings to be healing, life-generating, and sustaining rather than life-threatening, we must simply learn how to express them appropriately. As with a fire, we must create a safe and constructive environment in which they can burn healthily.

Our repressed anger can be compared to a powerful river that has been dammed up. If we have stopped the river cold, allowing very little or no flow at all, our land will be dry and parched. And we can bet that eventually, when the pressure gets to be too much, our dam will come crashing down, and the water—our blocked and repressed life force—will come raging out, sweeping away everything in its path. Because we have already held back so much of our life force, we must learn very carefully structured, very safe ways to release it. Eventually, when we have released enough of our repressed feelings, the natural flow of current events and the whole range of emotions that attend them can move through us less intensely.

A safe and healthy environment, or "container," for our feelings involves their appropriate expression and appropriate reception within agreed upon parameters. In the Imago Process, there are three processes for the appropriate containment of charged feelings. In this session, you will work with two of them. The third, "Container Days," will be introduced in the final session.

The Container processes are essentially Couple's Dialogues specifically structured to express and receive anger and frustration. In the Containment processes, as in the Couple's Dialogue, there is a Sender and a Receiver— only in these processes, one partner expresses at a time. Healing can occur only if expressed feelings are fully received and the Receiver is not reactive to what is expressed. The main difference between the Couple's Dialogue and the Containment processes is that the Receiver does not (necessarily) send his or her own message back when the Sender is finished.

The first of these Containment processes is called the *Container Transaction*. It is a brief exercise used when one partner is mildly frustrated or angry. It is essentially a Couple's Dialogue transaction (one Sender, one Receiver, no switch) followed by an optional translation of the Frustration into Behavior Change Requests. It is a short process (3 to 10 minutes) used for the immediate discharge of negative feeling before it builds up. A request for behavior change may or may not be made, depending on the needs of the expressive (Sender) partner.

The *Container Exercise* is used for the safe and constructive expression of highly charged feelings and enables us to connect our current frustration with stored-up feelings from our childhood. It allows full expression and reception of *all* the sender's feelings connected to or triggered by a present behavior and may take 30 to 45 minutes.

Please note that these times are approximate. Both Containment processes are over when the Sender is complete with the communication, not when a particular amount of time has passed. Like the Container Transaction, the Container Exercise begins with a Couple's Dialogue transaction and includes Behavior Change Requests. However, in a Container Exercise, translating the Frustration into a Desire and a Behavior Change Request is *not* optional. After a highly charged communication of what we *don't* like, it is important that we let our partners know what we *do* want instead.

The middle part of the Container Exercise is carefully structured to allow for a safe "explosion" of intense feelings; connecting the feelings triggered now with feelings and experiences from childhood; and allowing other, softer feelings that have been hidden behind the anger to come out. The shift from an initial explosion of feelings (usually anger-related) that energetically move outward to an implosion of softer feelings (sadness, hurt, tears) that energetically move inward happens naturally. Our wounds them-selves feel soft; our *response* to being wounded, usually some degree of anger or rage, feels hard. A great part of the value in safely releasing rage is that it allows us to touch and feel our deep wounds, which need to be felt in order to be healed.

Both partners need safety in a Containment process. As the expressive partner, your need for safety is more obvious: you need safety in order to go against your powerful directives *not* to express yourself fully, and you need the safety of knowing how to express your intense feelings without hurting yourself or others. As the Containing partner, your need for safety is less obvious but no less important: you need to know you will not be attacked or harmed in any way—physically, emotionally, or mentally—in order to be able to stay fully and lovingly present for your partner. In all of these Con-tainment processes, *both partners create the safe and appropriate container.* Making the following agreements creates a safe environment:

- All expressions of angry feelings are done by appointment only. Requests for appointments are granted as soon as possible, preferably immediately.
- Both partners stay fully present until the process is completed.
- Neither partner causes any bodily harm to himself or herself or to his or her partner.
- Neither partner destroys any property.

Making an appointment allows the receiving partner to go into contain-ment mode so he or she can safely hear the sending partner's communica-tion.

As the Sender, or expressive partner, you create safety by honoring the following guidelines:

- As much a possible, use "I" language, language that describes your experience and feelings.
- Describe the BEHAVIORS that are upsetting to you.
- Do *not* call your partner abusive names or criticize his or her charac-ter or motivation.

Describing your feelings in "I" language, and therefore owning your own experience rather than blaming your partner for it, helps your partner hear what you have to say. For example, it would be easier, safer, and more constructive for your partner to hear "I feel ignored when you say that," rather than "You always make me feel terrible when you say things like that." You also help your partner hear you by describing behavior rather than calling him or her abusive names or criticizing his or her character or motivation. For example, "I am angry that you were late and didn't call," rather than "You're such a jerk. You're so unreliable. You don't even care enough about me to call."

As the receiver or containing partner, you create safety by firmly anchoring yourself in containment mode:

- Visualize your partner as a wounded child.
- Remember that your partner's feelings are rooted in his or her childhood. Your actions have triggered your partner into his or her childhood wounds, but you are not the original cause of the hurt and therefore not the target.
- Listen to your partner with empathy, care, and compassion.
- Receive your partner's communication, rather than responding to it.

As Containment replaces all other forms of disagreement or fighting and becomes how we habitually express and receive Frustrations, we learn that our partners' anger and other highly charged feelings won't hurt us. We also learn that our highly charged feelings won't hurt us, and they won't hurt our partners, either. We develop a clearer sense of boundaries, learning that we don't have to be entwined in our partners' emotional states. We find we have less negative response to our partner's upset or angry feelings. We become more empathic with our partners. We begin to allow ourselves and our partners fuller expression of emotions.

There is no such thing as a person who never gets angry. There are people who repress and deny their rage, but there is no one living who doesn't have it. We fear that what is inside of us is dark, ugly, and overpowering. Yet once we gain the courage to wrestle with this fear and fully express our feelings, we learn an astonishing thing: what is hiding inside us is our own blocked life energy. It is love, it is light, and releasing this energy is the ultimate purpose of love relationships.

EXERCISE

The Container Transaction

Suggested time: 20–30 minutes.

△   The Container Transaction is essentially a Couple's Dialogue transaction about a minor Frustration, optionally followed by translating the Frustration into Behavior Change Requests. Practice the Container Transaction once in each role (Sender, Receiver) before moving on to the Container Exercise.

STEP 1.

Decide who will be the Sender and will express a Frustration and who will be the Receiver and will contain the Frustration.

STEP 2.

Sender: Pick a minor Frustration as the subject of the exercise. Ask your partner for an appointment to express your anger or Frustration.

For example: "I am upset, and I would like to make an appointment to express that with you. When can we do that?"

- Tell your partner how angry you are. The intensity of your emotion determines how much time you will need to express it.

STEP 3.

Receiver: Agree to receive your partner's communication in a Container Transaction as soon as possible, preferably immediately.

- Use your partner's information about how upset or angry he or she is to help you allow an appropriate amount of time, anywhere from 3 to 10 minutes for mild Frustrations to 30 or 45 minutes or longer for a highly charged Container Transaction. These times are approximate. A Container Transaction is over when the Sender is finished with the communication, not when a particular amount of time has passed.

STEP 4.
Receiver: Take a few deep breaths, and go into Container mode:

- Visualize your partner as a wounded child.
- Remember that your partner's feelings are rooted in his or her childhood. Your actions have triggered your partner into his or her Childhood Wounds, but you are not the original cause of the hurt and therefore not the target.
- Listen to your partner with empathy.

STEP 5.
Receiver: Indicate when you are ready.

STEP 6.
Sender and Receiver: Create a safe container for your feelings. Honor the following agreements:

- Both partners stay fully present until the process is completed.
- Neither partner causes any bodily harm to himself or herself or to his or her partner.
- Neither partner destroys any property.

STEP 7.
Sender: State your Frustration as briefly, simply, and directly as possible.

For example: "I am angry that you worked late every night this week and we didn't have even one dinner together."

- Start your communication with "I" followed by a feeling (remember that a feeling can usually be expressed with one word—*angry, hurt, ignored,* etc.) and then a description of the hurtful or frustrating behavior.
- Create a safe container for your communication. Honor the following guidelines:

  1. Describe the behaviors that are upsetting you.
  2. Do *not* call your partner abusive names or criticize his or her character or motivation.

- Say: "I am angry that you worked late every night this week." Rather than: "You're a workaholic! You're so cut off from your feelings. You don't love me enough to have dinner with me once a week."

STEP 8.
Receiver: Mirror your partner's communication, and ask for clarification until he or she is satisfied that you have fully heard his or her Frustration. Validate and Empathize with your partner's communication.

- Acknowledging your partner's anger does not mean that you agree with him or her or that you accept blame. It means you understand that your partner is angry. All you are doing is affirming his or her emotional state.
- Remember to receive your partner's communication, rather than responding to it.

STEP 9.
Sender: If you want to, make a Behavior Change Request of your partner.

For example: "I would like you to set aside one evening a week for us to have dinner and spend time together, no matter what. I would like our evening together to begin no later than 7:00."

- Remember, a Behavior Change Request is positively expressed, very specific, and quantified as much as possible.

STEP 10.
Receiver: If you can, tell your partner that you will grant the Behavior Change Request. If you cannot grant the request now, add it to your list. Ask your partner if he or she feels finished for now.

STEP 11.
Sender: If you feel finished for now, say so, and thank your partner for receiving your communication.

- If the Sender can reply yes, then the Container Transaction is complete.
- If the Sender has more to say about his or her original Frustration, repeat the process until he or she is finished.

STEP 12.
Receiver: Thank your partner for openly communicating his or her feelings.

STEP 13.
Sender and Receiver: Add all Behavior Change Requests to both of your lists in the appropriate places.

STEP 14.

Switch roles, and repeat the Container Transaction, Steps 2 through 13.

STEP 15.

Have a brief Couple's Dialogue sharing your feelings and thoughts about the Container Transaction.

EXERCISE

The Container Exercise

Suggested time: 1 hour and 15 minutes.

△   The first few times you practice this exercise (now and as a Between-Session Assignment), keep your Study Guide handy, carefully following along with each step.

STEP 1.

Warning! Read the entire exercise, the "Safety Agreements and Guidelines for All Containment Processes" on page 191, the "Container Exercise Outline" on pages 192–193, and the Container Exercise sample on pages 194–196 now before beginning. Do not proceed until you have completed Step 1.

STEP 2.

If there are any instructions that are unclear to you, briefly discuss them with your partner to clarify them.

STEP 3.

Decide who will be the Sender and who will be the Receiver.

1. MAKE AN APPOINTMENT. (The number corresponds to the Container Exercise Outline.)

STEP 4.

Very important! Sender: Pick a *moderately* charged Frustration to practice the exercise with. (Save your highly charged issues until you are more familiar with the process.) Ask your partner for an appointment to express your anger.

For example: "I am really angry with you, and I would like to make an appointment for a Container Exercise. When can we do that?"

- Tell your partner how upset you are so he or she can allow an appropriate amount of time for you to fully express yourself.

STEP 5.
Receiver: Agree to receive your partner's communication in a Container Exercise as soon as possible, preferably immediately.

- If your partner has not specified how angry he or she is, ask, so you can allow an appropriate amount of time—20 to 30 minutes for a moderately charged Frustration and 30 to 45 minutes for a highly charged Frustration. These times are approximate. A Container Exercise is over when the Sender is finished with the communication, not when a particular amount of time has passed.

STEP 6.
Receiver: Take a few deep breaths, and go into Containment mode.

- Visualize your partner as a wounded child.
- Remember that your partner's feelings are rooted in his or her childhood. Your actions have triggered your partner into his or her Childhood Wound, but you are not the original cause of the hurt and therefore not the target.
- Listen to your partner with empathy, compassion, and care.

STEP 7.
Receiver: Indicate when you are ready.

STEP 8.
Sender and Receiver: Create a safe container for your feelings. Honor the following agreements:

- Both partners stay fully present until the process is completed.
- Neither partner causes any bodily harm to himself or herself or to his or her partner.
- Neither partner destroys any property.

2. COUPLE'S DIALOGUE TRANSACTION

STEP 9.
Sender: Identify the trigger. State your Frustration as briefly, simply, and directly as possible.

For example: "I am angry that you were anxious and impatient with me tonight when we were preparing for our guests."

- Start your communication with "I" followed by a feeling (remember, a feeling can usually be expressed with one word—*angry, hurt, ignored,* etc.) and then a description of the hurtful or frustrating behavior.
- Keep this initial communication simple and direct.
- Create a safe container for your communication. Honor the following guidelines:

1. Describe the BEHAVIORS that are upsetting you.
2. Do *not* call your partner abusive names or criticize his or her character or motivation.

- Say: "I am angry about the way you treated me when we were getting ready for our guests." Rather than: "You're such a nag. You're so bossy. You want everything done your way."

STEP 10.

Receiver: Mirror your partner's communication, and ask for clarification until he or she is satisfied that you have fully heard his or her Frustration. Validate and Empathize with your partner's communication.

- Acknowledging your partner's anger does not mean that you agree with him or her or that you accept blame. It means you understand that your partner is angry. All you are doing is affirming his or her emotional state.

3. EXPLOSION OF FEELINGS

STEP 11.

Sender: Once your initial statement has been received, fully express all of your feelings and responses to the Frustration, honoring the "Safety Agreements and Guidelines for All Containment Processes," page 191.

- As much as possible, use "I" language that describes your experience and your feelings.

Say: "I stop having fun when you ask me to do too many things at once too fast. And I get really frustrated when I do something you ask me to and then you don't like it or it's not good enough and you do it over. Then I feel like not participating at all, and I wish nobody was coming over." Rather than: "You make it no fun when you want me to do too much too fast. Then you make me feel like not helping at all when you do something over that I just did. You make me wish nobody was coming to visit."

STEP 12.
Receiver: Stay in Containment mode as you listen to your partner's explosion of feelings.

- You heal your partner by allowing him or her to express his or her feelings.
- This explosion of feelings may go on for a while, anywhere from 5 to 15 minutes or more.
- The following list is included to remind you to receive rather than respond in a charged situation. Do not:

  - Ask questions other than the ones specifically included in the process.
  - Countercriticize: "Well, you had a negative attitude, too."
  - Analyze your partner: "You feel like that because your mother used to make you help in the kitchen when company was coming over."
  - Judge your partner: "You are being childish and overreacting to this."
  - Invalidate your partner's experience: "You shouldn't be so mad. We had a great time, and the house looked great."
  - Deny your partner's perception: "I was not impatient with you. I was just being efficient."

STEP 13.
Sender: Connect your current feelings with childhood experiences and feelings.

- The connection may happen naturally as part of your explosion.
- As your explosion is winding down, you may wish to fill of the blanks of the following sentence to help you connect what you are feeling now with your original wound. "I don't like it when you . . . I feel . . . and I react by . . . to hide my fear of . . ."
- Receiver: If your partner's charge is winding down and he or she has not made the connection to childhood, you can coach him or her by asking, "Does this remind you of anything in your childhood?"

  - Ask this question when your partner's charge is winding down. Never interrupt your partner's initial burst of feelings.
  - Ask the question as it is written, with compassion and care.
  - Do not use it as a weapon to prove anything to you partner. Use it to help your partner connect the present frustration or hurt with his or her childhood wound.
  - Do not tell your partner what you think is going on. Only ask the question.

STEP 14.
Sender: Make sure your partner hears you accurately.

- Ask your partner, at any time as you are expressing your feelings, to Mirror an important point.
- Or express your feelings without interruption, and then ask your partner to review the important points with you when you are done. Restate the important points, one by one, allowing your partner to Mirror each one until he or she has heard you accurately. Ask your partner to offer important points he or she remembers that you may have missed, and use Mirroring to clarify them.
- *This is not a test.* Help each other make sure the key points, feelings, and thoughts have been fully and accurately communicated.
- You may also choose not to ask your partner to Mirror anything.
- It is possible that you may not wish to review key points until after Step 15.

4. IMPLOSION OF FEELINGS

STEP 15.
Sender: You may eventually find yourself naturally shifting from harder, more angry feelings to softer, more hurt or sad feelings. Allow yourself to feel these feelings deeply and express them as fully as possible.

- Cry if you feel like crying.
- If it feels good to you, allow your partner to comfort you.
- It is possible, if the Sender's feelings are not so highly charged, that an implosion may not happen.

STEP 16.
Receiver: When the Sender's feelings soften, provide physical holding if your partner wants it, along with your empathy, compassion, and care.

5. OPTIONAL BREAK

STEP 17.
Sender: At this point, you may wish to take a break, either with your partner or separately. If you do take a break, give it a time limit—5 to 30 minutes—and then come back to finish

the exercise. Receiver: You may wish to ask the sender if he or she would like to take a break.

6. Make Behavior Change Requests

STEP 18.
Sender: Translate your Frustration into a Desire, and then make any Behavior Change Requests related to the triggering behavior.

- Receiver: You can coach your partner at this stage by asking, "What is it that you desire of me?" And when that is answered, "What specifically could I do to satisfy that Desire?"
- It is important after a highly charged expression of negative feelings to clarify and communicate the deep Desire that needs to be satisfied, as well as the specific ways to do that.

STEP 19.
Receiver: Commit to at least one of your partner's Behavior Change Requests, or offer an alternative.

STEP 20.
Sender: Thank your partner for the Behavior Change Request he or she has committed to making. If your partner has offered an alternative, accept that appreciatively as a step toward satisfying your Desire.

STEP 21.
Receiver: Ask the Sender if he or she feels finished for now.

STEP 22.
Sender: If you feel finished for now, say so, and thank your partner for receiving your communication.

- If you can reply yes, then the Container Exercise is complete.
- If you have more to say about your original Frustration, repeat appropriate portions of the exercise until your communication is finished. You may wish to have a simple Container Transaction—that is, a Couple's Dialogue transaction followed by optional Behavior Change Requests.

STEP 23.

Receiver: Thank your partner for fully and openly communicating his or her feelings.

7. HIGH-ENERGY PLAY

STEP 24

Sender: Initiate some high-energy play.

For example: bicycling, making love, dancing, taking a shower together.

STEP 25.

Receiver: Participate actively in the high-energy play.

STEP 26.

Sender and Receiver: Add all Behavior Change Requests to both of your lists in the appropriate places.

- If absolutely no agreement can be reached about behavior changes to be made, the Receiver adds the requests to his or her Behavior Change Requests from the "My Partner" list in the Appendix anyway, pages 263–266.

STEP 27.

Have a Couple's Dialogue about the Container Exercise and your experience while doing it.

STEP 28.

On another day, switch roles and repeat the Container Exercise, Steps 4 through 26.

SAFETY AGREEMENTS AND GUIDELINES
FOR ALL CONTAINMENT PROCESSES

Create a safe and appropriate Container for your highly charged feelings by honoring these agreements and guidelines. If you have *any* concerns about doing this exercise with your partner, or if you have ever been physically violent with each other, please go to www.imagorelationships.org and ask for a referral to an IMAGO therapist, or go to your therapist, if you have one.

Safety Agreements

- All expressions of angry feelings are done by appointment only. Appointments are granted as soon as possible, preferably immediately.
- Both partners stay fully present until the process is completed.
- Neither partner causes any bodily harm to himself or herself or to his or her partner.
- Neither partner destroys any property.

Guidelines for the Sender/Expressing Partner:

- Describe the BEHAVIORS that are upsetting to you.
- Do *not* call your partner abusive names or criticize his or her character or motivation.
- As much as possible, use "I" language that describes your experience and what you feel.

Guidelines for the Receiver/Containing Partner:

- Listen to your partner with Empathy.
- Visualize your partner as a wounded child.
- Remember that your partner's feelings are rooted in his or her childhood. Your actions have triggered your partner into his or her Childhood Wound, but you are not the original cause of the hurt and therefore not the target.
- Remember to RECEIVE your partner's communication, rather than responding to it.

The Container Exercise Outline

1. Make an appointment

Receiver: Go into Containment mode.

2. Couple's Dialogue Transaction

Sender: Make an initial statement of Frustration.

Receiver: Mirror, Validate, and Empathize.

3. Explosion of Feelings

Sender: Fully express feelings in "I" language.

Receiver: Listen with Empathy.

During Explosion or Implosion

Connect current Frustration with childhood.

Sender: Make connection with childhood feelings.

Receiver: If necessary, ask, "Does this remind you of anything in your childhood?" to help the Sender make the connection.

Review important points.

Sender: Ask the Receiver to Mirror important points along the way.

Sender: Review your communication at the end by restating important points and allowing the Receiver to mirror them. Also, ask the Receiver to offer important points for clarification.

4. Implosion of Feelings

Sender: Feel and express softer feelings.

Receiver: Provide holding.

5. Optional Break

The Sender may request it or not. The Receiver can ask if the Sender feels the need for one.

6. Make Behavior Change Requests

Sender: Translate your Frustration into a Desire and Behavior Change Requests.

Receiver: If necessary, coach Sender by asking, "What is it that you desire of me?" and "What specifically could I do to satisfy that Desire?"

Receiver: Commit to one behavior change, or offer an alternative.

Receiver: Check with the Sender to make sure he or she is finished.

Both partners: Thank each other for participating.

7. High-Energy Play

Sender: Initiate high-energy play.

Receiver: Actively participate.

CONTAINER EXERCISE
Sample

Greg: *Sandy, I'm really upset, and I want to clear the air as soon as possible. When can we do that?*

Sandy: *I can do it now. Just give me a minute to orient myself.* (Sandy goes into Containment mode.) *Okay, I'm ready.*

Greg: *I am furious with you for what you said tonight to Bill and Sharon about having kids!*

Sandy: *You're really mad about me talking to Sharon and Bill about having children. Is that what you said?*

Greg: *Yes, almost. I'm especially upset about you speaking for me and saying I was considering it.*

Sandy: *You're angry that I talked to them about our having children and especially angry that I spoke for you. Is that better?*

Greg: *Yes, and you made it sound as if I'm feeling something that I'm not.*

Sandy: *And I didn't accurately convey what you are feeling about it. How's that?*

Greg: *Yes, that's it.*

Sandy: *Okay. I get that you are really upset. I imagine it must have been hard to hold this in until now. Thank you for doing that.*

Greg: *You're welcome. So, I felt really embarrassed to hear you talking about having children when it's such an unresolved issue between us. I don't want to talk to other people about it until we are more resolved. Or until I'm more comfortable about it. I don't want you talking about it. It feels like hanging our dirty laundry out in public. And what really makes me angry is that we have been, I thought we had been, communicating really well about it. I am not ready. You telling them that I'm considering it sounds to me as if you're saying I've made a decision. Or as if you've made that decision for me. As if you're not listening to me. As if I don't really have a choice about this at all. I mean, what would you do if I said I really don't ever want to do this? You've said that would be okay. But tonight I didn't feel like that. I felt there's only one choice I can make and that you've already made that choice for me! Don't put words in my mouth! I hate that! And let me speak for myself about this—and everything, for that matter. We are a couple, and I love you, and I'm here, but I have a mind and a mouth of my own. It makes me so* angry!!! Aaaghgh! *Okay. So, what really upset me was your telling them what I am thinking. Will you mirror that so I know you hear me?*

Sandy: *You really don't like it when I speak for you or answer questions about what you're thinking. Is that it?*

Greg: *Yes. Will you do the part about why I don't like that?*

Sandy: *Uh, just a second, let me think. Okay, you don't like it because it feels too personal in public? And because we're not clear about it yet, and why else?*

Greg: *Yes to both of those, but most importantly because I felt as if you weren't listening to me when I said I wasn't ready.*

Sandy: *When I told them you were considering having children, you felt as if I didn't really hear that you are not ready to do it yet. Did I get it?*

Greg: *Yeah, and because, I guess, I'm afraid of what will happen if I don't want to have kids. I'm afraid, I guess, that you'll leave. That you want to have kids more than you want to be with me.* (Greg has moved from being angry to feeling a deep fear, and he cries. Sandy holds him. When he is calmer, she coaches him.)

Sandy: *Does this remind you of anything in your childhood?*

Greg: *I guess . . . well, my mother loves me better than my father. When I came along, she just stopped paying attention to my dad and gave all her love to me. She was always defending me against him and giving him a hard time whenever he said anything to me at all. He was really left out. I guess what I'm really afraid of is that if we do have kids, you'll love them more than me, and I'll end up like my dad, the outcast, the bad guy. Oh, God.* (Greg cries a little more.)

Sandy: *Do you need a break for a while before we go on?*

Greg: *Yeah, maybe. Can we take about five minutes off? I'm just going to go outside to clear my head.*

Sandy: *Okay.*

Greg: (Five minutes later.) *Where are we?*

Sandy: *What do you desire of me around our process about having children or around my talking about it?*

Greg: *Thanks. Umm, I want you . . . I want to feel as if I really can make up my own mind about this. And as if you will support whatever decision I make. And that if I choose to have kids, it's because I really want to, not because I'm afraid of what will happen if I don't, or do for that matter. Okay. Let me restate that. I would like to feel supported and fully loved no matter what decision I make. I want you to really let me make my own choice here.*

Sandy: *Okay. And specific behavior changes I can make to satisfy that desire. Three of them.*

Greg: *I would like you to let me speak for myself about anything to do with children. I would like you to say, "Well, you'll have to ask Greg about what he's feeling or think-ing." I would like to hear you say you won't leave me if I decide not to have kids. I would like to have you remind me every time we talk about having kids that you are not going to abandon me for them. I want you to tell anyone who asks that we are talking about it and when we know what we want, we'll tell people. I want an unlimited amount of time to make my choice.*

Sandy: *Well, let's see. I can say that I won't leave you if you decide not to have kids, and I can remind you that if we do have children, I won't abandon you. I can commit to only speaking for myself and telling people to ask you about your thoughts and feel-ings. I can't do the unlimited amount of time thing—I guess that goes on my C list.*

Greg: *Okay. Thanks for that. That will make me feel more as if I really can make my own choice around this.*

Sandy: *Are you finished for now?*

Greg: *Yeah. I think so. Want to take a shower together?*

Sandy: *That sounds good. Let's do that.*

STEP 29.
Read the Points to Remember together now.

STEP 30.
Answer the Review Questions together, noting your answers in the spaces provided.

STEP 31.
Read the Between-Session Assignments together now.

STEP 32.
If you have not scheduled a regular time for your sessions, make an appointment for your next session now. (Note: Session 11 is 2 hours and 15 minutes long.)

POINTS TO REMEMBER

- Appropriate expression of anger is the key to regaining our joyful aliveness.

- Both partners participate in creating the safety of a Containment process.

- The key skill for you to learn as the expressive partner, or Sender, in a Containment process is to own your feelings and experience by using "I" language, rather than blaming or criticizing your partner.

- The key skill for you to learn as the Containing partner, or Receiver, is to receive rather than respond.

- The combination of appropriate Containment (expression and reception) of our feelings and granting Behavior Change Requests to meet each other's needs heals our deepest wounds.

REVIEW QUESTIONS

Why is it so difficult for us to express our anger and other intense feelings?

How do we benefit by substituting appropriate Containment for all spontaneous conflict, disagreement, and fighting?

Why is safety during the expression of anger so important?

Why is it important to own our feelings and experience by using "I" language?

Why is it important to receive our partners' feelings rather than respond to them?

BETWEEN-SESSION ASSIGNMENTS
1. This is a very full session. If you do not complete the entire session in the time you have allotted, make an appointment to complete it together as soon as possible.
2. Use the Container Transaction to deal with your everyday Frustrations with your partner.
3. Reread this entire session before Session 11, plus the additional sample Container Exercises in the Appendix on pages 267–272.

4. **Practice the Container Exercise at least two times this week (only one in a day) with moderate Frustrations. Alternate roles so you can play both Sender and Receiver twice. Have a brief Couple's Dialogue after each practice to share your feelings and thoughts about your experience.**

   - Follow along with Steps 4 through 26 in your study guide as you practice. Remember, you are dealing with highly charged emotions. Practice this new skill with care and attention until it becomes habit.

   - If you practice this exercise regularly for three weeks, you will be able to easily contain the high voltage when it comes along. You can start right now. Don't wait until after something breaks to look at the manual and figure out how it works.

   - As the Sender, focus on owning your communication by using "I" language. As the Receiver, focus on listening with empathy, care, and compassion and visualizing your partner as a wounded child.

5. **Have a Couple's Dialogue this week about Re-Romanticizing your relationship. Include your feelings about Caring Behaviors, Surprises, and Fun and the effect these exercises have had on your relationship.**

6. **In *Getting the Love You Want,* review Chapter 2, "Childhood Wounds," and "Hidden Sources of Knowledge" in Chapter 9, "Increasing Your Knowledge of Yourself and Your Partner" before Session 11.**

7. **Continue:**

   - Add to any of your lists as new thoughts occur to you. Inform your partner of additions that apply to him or her.

   - Grant your partner at least one easy Behavior Change Request this week. Note the date it is granted next to the request on the form in your Appendix.

   - Do at least one high-energy Fun activity with your partner every day this week.

   - Give your partner another Surprise at an unexpected time this week, and enjoy his or her response. Be sure to record the date you gave the Surprise. Record Surprises received from your partner, with dates.

   - Give your partner at least one Caring Behavior every day this week.

   - Before Session 11, have a Couple's Dialogue with your partner about the Exits you have closed or reduced so far, and choose at least one more Exit to close or reduce.

   - Close or reduce the Exit(s) you have agreed upon.

   - One day this week, write down three things that your partner does that please you (separate from granted Behavior Change Requests, Caring Behaviors, Surprises, and Fun), and share them with him or her at the end of the day. Use the form in the Appendix, pages 240–242. Include the date in column 1.

- Visualize your partner as a wounded child, especially in conflict situations and when he or she behaves in ways that frustrate you.
- Use the Couple's Dialogue as a habitual part of your communication with your partner.
- Read your Mutual Relationship Vision together at least once before Session 11.

8. **Remember:**
   - Give your partner the gifts of Caring Behaviors, Surprises, and granting Behavior Change Requests regardless of how you feel about your partner and regardless of how many gifts your partner gives you.
   - Acknowledge your partner appreciatively for each gift he or she gives you—Behavior Change Requests, Surprises, Caring Behaviors, and any others.
   - Engage in high-energy Fun activities on a daily basis.
   - Continue, even if you feel resistance to any of the exercises, to take the risk of doing something new and therefore perhaps uncomfortable, in order to create your Conscious Marriage. Remember, the more difficult a particular exercise seems to you, the more potential it contains for growth.

Self-Integration

REVIEW in *Getting the Love You Want*
Chapter 2, "Childhood Wounds," and "Hidden Sources of Knowledge" in Chapter 9, "Increasing Your Knowledge of Yourself and Your Partner."

TIME FRAME
2 hours and 15 minutes.

OBJECTIVES

- Identify your Lost, False, Disowned, and True Selves.
- Integrate your Lost and Disowned Selves into your self-image.
- Turn chronic complaints and criticisms into a constructive source of information and healing.
- Experience your full aliveness by recovering your True Self.

THEORY
As we have seen, we are wounded during our socialization as we are given direct or indirect messages that parts of us are unacceptable. Our caretakers and society reward or ignore certain of our talents, aptitudes, behaviors, thoughts, or feelings. We are told how to feel, think, and act and how *not* to feel, think, and act. Most of our socialization, however, happens by example. We observe the choices our caretakers (and, later, others) make, the freedoms and pleasures they allow themselves, what they praise and what they reject, the talents they develop, the abilities they ignore, and the rules they follow.

In response to all of these messages, we make adjustments, changing what doesn't meet with acceptance, and develop an image that pleases. We repress parts of our *True Self*—our original whole being—in order to be accepted and survive. These repressed aspects of our original self—the natural qualities, abilities, and feelings that we remove from our awareness—are called the *Lost Self*. We still possess these traits, but they are buried, no longer part of our conscious self-image. Let's look at Ellen's story as an example:

> Ellen's parents were not openly comfortable with sexuality. Nothing negative was directly said, but sex and sexuality were never mentioned. Ellen's early messages about sexuality came from observing her parents together. She noticed that they were comfortable with expressing certain kinds of affection between them but uncomfortable with others; they seemed to have rules about what was and wasn't okay for the children to see. As Ellen's sexual energy became more apparent in her preteen years, her father became uncomfortable around her. He was still affectionate but also withdrawn, not as exuberantly, openly loving as he had been before. Ellen's mother was also not overtly negative, but she subtly warned Ellen to "be careful," to "watch herself with boys so she didn't get into trouble." Ellen received the message that there was something wrong with her, something wrong with these new feelings she was having. Unconsciously, she concluded that if she wanted to keep her parents' love, she had better get rid of what was "wrong" or at least hide it. She has taken her parents' message to heart and feels that it is bad to be openly, exuberantly, joyfully sexual. As an adult, she says of herself, "I'm not very sexy. Never have been. I like to be affectionate, but I just can't be sexy."

When you say that you "can't think," "can't dance," "can't have orgasms," "aren't very creative," you are identifying your Lost Self. Your Lost Self includes both consciously suppressed, unacceptable, or ridiculed parts of yourself that you are aware of but keep hidden and unconsciously repressed, deeply inhibited parts of yourself that you are unaware of.

To camouflage or compensate for those parts of your being that you had to repress and to protect you from further injury around not getting your needs met, you create a *False Self*. You develop new traits to get or keep your parents' love and to be more acceptable to society. You adopt some traits directly from your caretakers that seem to get them what they want. You create an image that you feel will protect you and be approved of. Your

False Self is an alias, an assumed identity that helps you maneuver in the world. To continue Ellen's story:

> Ellen became a tomboy, developing a rough-and-tumble, one-of-the-guys outlet for her sexuality. She can safely express a certain kind of affection, playing with boys as one of them, rather than risking the uncomfortable withdrawal or focus of attention that being a girl would cause. As an adult, Ellen is a highly effective business executive operating as an equal among men. In her marriage, Ellen is comfortable with certain areas of affection and intimacy—she is a great pal and a strong partner. Yet open, exuberant, joyful, sexy, feminine intimacy is very difficult and threatening to her.

Paradoxically, your False Self can continue to wound you by "protecting" you from getting your deepest needs met. Again, let's look at Ellen:

> Ellen deeply needs to express her exuberant, joyful, feminine sexuality and to have it appreciated and accepted. However, she has created an image of tough affection that, on one hand, protects her from being hurt by disapproval again and, on the other hand keeps her from receiving the very love and approval she needs.

Last, you find that some parts of the new False Self that you have created are also perceived as negative by others and are therefore unacceptable. Because your False Self protects you, however, you cannot just get rid of these parts, so you deny them. These denied parts become your *Disowned Self,* the negative parts of your False Self that others recognize in you, but you refuse to acknowledge in yourself. It would be painful to acknowledge these disowned traits because you created your False Self to be good, to be acceptable. It is confusing and hurtful when parts of it are perceived as bad.

> Thus, when Ellen is accused by her partner of not having enough fun and not being sexy enough and is teased about her no-frills wardrobe, she feels hurt and angry. She perceives herself as strong and practical. It is true that she *is* strong and practical, *and* she has also substituted practicality and being strong for soft, open, feminine, joyful, sexy fun.

You can identify your Disowned Self when you are repeatedly accused of having negative character traits that you feel are being misunderstood. For example, you might be accused of being cold and distant and feel misunderstood because you perceive yourself as strong and independent; or you might be perceived as weak and needy when you feel you are sensitive. You may indeed be strong, independent, or sensitive, but—as your partner and friends will testify—you are also cold, distant, weak, and needy.

Of the True Self, the Lost Self, the False Self, and the Disowned Self, you are only aware of what is left of your True Self and the parts of your False Self that you have not disowned. These form your personality, the way you would describe yourself to others. Your Lost and Disowned Selves hover outside your normal level of awareness, periodically illuminated by your partner's criticisms and behavior change requests. Although your Lost and Disowned Selves conflict with who you perceive yourself to be, they are nonetheless active in you. Until you own these parts and integrate them into your picture of who you are, you are operating at cross purposes with yourself.

In your Imago partner, you have, among other things, fallen in love with your *Missing Self*—your Lost and Disowned Selves combined. Intimate commitment forces you to own what you deny in yourself because you cannot indefinitely mask from your partner the traits you are able to camouflage in public. You also cannot expect your partner to make up for the traits missing in yourself. Since you view these parts as negative or dangerous, you relate to them by externalizing them—either annexing your Lost Self traits or projecting your Disowned Self traits onto your partner. (Projection is taking disowned qualities that are incompatible with your self-image and attributing them to someone else.) Then you criticize your partner for having them, and they become a source of conflict in your relationship.

You can turn these chronic criticisms of each other into a rich source of useful information by assuming there is some truth about yourself in your criticisms of your partner. The things you hate most are often true of you. Also, there is some truth about you in your partner's criticism of you. You can ask, "What truth is there that I don't want to see in my partner's criticism of me?" You can ask, "In what way is my criticism of my partner also true of me?"—keeping in mind that you may exhibit these traits differently from the way your partner does. Often, when a criticism is not a description of a disowned negative part of yourself, it is a description of a more deeply unconscious part of your Lost Self. It is a wish to be more like the trait you are criticizing your partner for. Let's return to Ellen's story as an example:

When Ellen and her husband, Gary, first met, one of the qualities that attracted Ellen to Gary was his exuberant and fun-loving sexuality, his lighthearted and open lovemaking, and his enthusiastic, joyful acknowledgment of her attractiveness to him. One of Ellen's chronic complaints about Gary is that he is too openly, exuberantly sexual "all the time." This is a disguised wish on Ellen's part to be more free and joyous in her own sexuality, to reclaim this part of her Lost Self. One of Gary's criticisms of Ellen is that she is sexually uninterested and unresponsive. Ellen feels she is not uninterested and unresponsive; she is just affectionate and sensible—which is true. However, Gary is identifying a part of Ellen's Disowned Self. In response to her parents' messages about sexuality, Ellen became unresponsive to and uninterested in the kind of sexuality that seemed unacceptable to them.

The reclamation of all of your True Self is essential to your experience of genuine aliveness. You have *already* been enlarging your sense of your True Self by integrating your Disowned Self, dismantling your False Self, and recovering your Lost Self in the exercises you have completed with your partner in this study guide. The exercises in Session 11 are designed to help you become more aware of these changes.
Remember:

- Most of our partners' criticisms of us have some basis in reality.
- Many of our repetitious, emotional criticisms of our partners are disguised statements of our own unmet needs.
- Some of our repetitive, emotional criticisms of our partners may be an accurate description of a disowned part of ourselves.
- Some of our criticisms of our partners may help us identify our own Lost Selves.

EXERCISE

Self-Integration I—Identify Your Lost, False, and Disowned Selves

Suggested time: 30 minutes.

Δ　There is an abbreviated combined sample of this exercise and the next exercise (Self-Integration II) following their descriptions and worksheets on pages 214–215.

STEP 1.

In column 1 on the worksheet on pages 208–209, begin to identify your Lost Self by writing the circled positive traits of your Imago from Session 3, (page 54), and your Partner Profile from Session 5 (page 87).

STEP 2.

Add to this list any qualities of your partner that you at first liked and perceived as complementary to you and that later became annoying or frustrating.

For example: If you were first attracted to how expressive your partner was and later began to perceive him or her as emotionally excessive, you would include "expressive" on your list.

- Search "Frustrations with My Partner" from Session 5 for any qualities or behaviors that you initially liked, and include them on this list.

STEP 3.

In column 2 of the worksheet, identify your False Self. List the traits you had to develop in order to get or keep your parents' love and in order to be accepted socially. Include descriptions of the way you act today to try to get people to like you.

For example: "I try to do everything perfectly."

STEP 4.

In column 3, identify your Disowned Self by writing the circled negative traits of your IMAGO and your Partner Profile.

- As you copy the negative traits from your Imago and your Partner Profile, place a check mark next to the traits that are common to both exercises.

STEP 5.
Look over your Frustrations from Session 5, and ask yourself in what way each of these criticisms might also be true of you. Include any of these negative qualities or behaviors that might describe a part of you that you don't like.

- This does not mean the Frustration is not a valid observation about your partner; it simply means it may also be a valid observation about you.
- Keep in mind that the way you exhibit these traits may be very different from the way your partner does.

STEP 6.
Add the circled negative traits from your partner's Imago and Partner Profile to your list.

- You can do this by writing these traits in your Study Guide as your partner reads them to you, and vice versa.
- Continue to place check marks next to the traits that are mentioned more than once. If you are reading for your partner, make sure to read all the circled traits, even if the same trait is mentioned more than once, so your partner can make note of it.

STEP 7.
Add to your description of your Disowned Self any repeated criticisms that family or friends have made of you, that are not already listed, continuing to note traits that are mentioned more than once.

SELF-INTEGRATION I

Identify Your Lost, False, and Disowned Selves

1 My Lost Self	2 My False Self	3 My Disowned Self

1 My Lost Self	2 My False Self	3 My Disowned Self

EXERCISE

Self-Integration II—Recover Your True Self
Suggested time: 1 hour and 15 minutes.

△   There is an abbreviated combined sample of this exercise and the previous exercise (Self-Integration I) following their descriptions and worksheets on pages 214–215.

STEP 1.

Look at your list of Lost Self traits, and think about the extent to which these positive qualities or attributes may be repressed parts of yourself.

- Have you ever been asked by your partner and other significant people in your life to develop these traits?
- Do you have a secret (perhaps very repressed) wish to be more like any of these traits?

STEP 2.

For the moment, assume that these traits do represent repressed aspects of yourself. On the worksheet in column 1 on page 213, describe your True Self, using these traits. Write each descriptive sentence as a short, positive statement in the present tense, beginning with the world "I" and ending with the trait.

For example: "I am expressive." Or, if one of the positive traits from your Imago or Partner Profile is "highly creative," you would write: "I am highly creative."

- Assume each of these traits is true of you, and include each one.

STEP 3

Look at your list of False Self traits. In column 1 of the worksheet, continuing where you left off in Step 2, describe the way you would be if you were free of each of these adaptive characteristics. Use simple, positive statements in the present tense that begin with "I."

For example: "I choose pleasure over perfection," or "I accept my mistakes."

- See the sample on pages 214–215.

STEP 4.

Look at your list of Disowned Self traits. Think about the extent to which these negative traits may be true of you.

- Has anyone, especially your partner, told you that you possess these traits?

STEP 5.

For the moment, assume that these traits are true of you. What would you be like if you did *not* have these traits? In column 1 of the worksheet, continuing where you left off in Step 3, write a description of the person you would be without these traits by converting each negative into a positive.

For example: If the negative trait is "cold" or "unavailable," you might say, "I am nurturing," or "I am loving," or "I am attentive."

- Write each descriptive sentence as a short, positive statement in the present tense beginning with the word "I."
- You may find that you think of more than one sentence per negative trait. Record them all.

STEP 6.

Add to your description of your True Self any traits that you value in yourself or that others value in you that have not been mentioned so far.

- These are the parts of your original being that survived your childhood nurturing deficits and your socialization.

STEP 7.

In column 2 of the worksheet, write one specific, positive behavior that would concretely express each positive trait of your True Self.

For example: If the positive trait is "I am nurturing," the new behavior might be "I give my partner a big hug at least three times day."

- Again, write each behavior in the present tense beginning with "I."
- Quantify your new behaviors whenever possible (how much, how often, etc.).
- Your partner may already have requested some of these behaviors from you.
- Some of the traits in column 1 may already be a part of your current behavior. If so, add a new behavior to the ways you currently express these traits.

STEP 8.

Read your Lost, False, and Disowned Selves and your True Self aloud to each other.

- Simply listen to each other's findings; do not comment.
- Remember, your Missing Self (your Lost and Disowned Selves combined) parts are a measure of your potential, and their recovery is essential to your experience of genuine aliveness.

STEP 9.

Have a brief Couple's Dialogue about both Self-Integration exercises, sharing your thoughts and feelings about what you discovered about yourself, *not* what you feel or think about what your partner discovered.

STEP 10.

Continue your Couple's Dialogue, now sharing your thoughts and feelings about what your partner discovered about himself or herself.

- Remember to use "I" language, owning your feelings and thoughts about what your partner discovered.
- Be supportive of yourself and your partner. Remember, your Missing Self parts are a measure of your potential.

STEP 11.

Pick one of the new behaviors to stretch into this week.

SELF-INTEGRATION II: RECOVER YOUR TRUE SELF

My True Self

1 Traits	2 New Behaviors

SELF-INTEGRATION

Combined Sample

My Lost Self	My True Self	New Behaviors

My False Self	My True Self	New Behaviors

My Disowned Self	My True Self	New Behaviors

SELF-INTEGRATION I & II

Combined Sample

My Lost Self	My True Self Traits	New Behaviors
expressive	I am expressive.	I let myself cry when I want to.
highly creative	I am highly creative.	I take painting classes.
listen well	I listen well.	I wait for people to completely finish their thoughts and allow a brief silence before I speak.

My False Self	My True Self Traits	New Behaviors
I try to do everything perfectly.	I choose pleasure over perfection.	I enjoy the way my partner cleans the living room when guests are coming.
	I accept my mistakes.	I have compassion for my own wounded child.
I am strong; I don't need anything from anyone.	I ask people to help me when I need it.	I ask my partner for help once a day.

My Disowned Self	My True Self Traits	New Behaviors
workaholic	I am fun-loving and playful.	I take one work afternoon off a week to do something fun with my partner.
cold	I am nurturing.	I give my partner a big hug at least three times a day.
	I am loving.	I tell my partner I love him or her at least once a day.
unavailable	I am fully present with my partner.	I tell my partner when I am angry with him or her.
take my partner for granted	I allow my partner to surprise me.	I approach my partner daily as if he or she is new and I do not know him or her.

EXERCISE

Visualize Your True Self (Guided Visualization)
Suggested time: 15 minutes.

△   If you do not have enough time to do this exercise during your session, do it as part of your Between-Session Assignments.

△   Read one sentence at a time. Complete the action described in the sentence, then move on to the next.

△   You can do this exercise separately, reading to yourself and moving at your own pace; or you can do it together, reading each sentence aloud and pacing yourselves together; or you can take turns, with one of you reading and the other doing the visualization. This last choice will lengthen the session by 15 minutes. If you choose this last option, establish some kind of signal for the person visualizing to give to the reader when he or she has completed the action in one sentence and is ready to move on to the next sentence.

△   You may wish to review "A Few Hints about Guided Visualization" on page 50 in Session 3.

STEP 1.
Reread your True Self traits and new behaviors.

- Make note especially of the traits or behaviors that are *not* part of your current behavior.

STEP 2.
Begin to get relaxed and comfortable.

- Take a good stretch, and let out a deep sigh.
- Get comfortable in your chair.
- Breathe deeply a few times, becoming more relaxed with each breath.
- When you are ready, allow yourself to close your eyes and relax even more.
- In your mind, slowly count down from 10 to 1, continuing to breathe deeply and relaxing more with each breath.

STEP 3.
When you are feeling comfortably relaxed, imagine yourself at some future time when the description you have just read of your True Self accurately and completely describes you.

- Especially include the traits and behaviors that are *not* part of your current reality.
- As if you were an actor in a movie, imagine being inside your True Self in this future time.

STEP 4.

As you continue to breathe and relax, look around you and notice what you see as your True Self.

- Use the following questions to help you see through the eyes of your True Self:
  ~What do you see around you?
  ~What are you doing?
  ~Who is with you?
  ~As your True Self, how do you see your partner?
  ~If you were to look in a mirror, what do you look like as your True Self?

STEP 5.

Even as you continue to notice what you see around you, begin to listen to what you hear as your True Self.

- Use the following questions to help you hear through the ears of your True Self.
  ~What sounds do you hear?
  ~What are you saying?
  ~What are people saying around you?
  ~What does your voice sound like?

STEP 6.

Continue to breathe and relax as you feel what it's like to be your True Self.

- Feel the difference between your True Self and the way you feel now.
  ~How do you feel about yourself?
  ~How do you feel about your partner?
  ~How do you feel about your life?

STEP 7.

When you have seen and heard and felt what it is like to be your True Self, slowly count back up from 1 to 10 in your mind, opening your eyes when you get to 10.

STEP 8.

On the worksheet on page 218, note what you saw and heard and felt as your True Self.

VISUALIZE YOUR TRUE SELF

I see . . . _____

_____

_____

_____

_____

_____

I hear . . . _____

_____

_____

_____

_____

_____

I feel . . . _____

_____

_____

_____

_____

_____

STEP 9.

Read the Points to Remember together now.

STEP 10.

Answer the Review Questions together, noting your answers in the spaces provided.

STEP 11.

Read the Between-Session Assignments together now.

STEP 12.

If you have not scheduled a regular time for your sessions, make an appointment for your final session now. (Note: Session 12 is 1 hour and 30 minutes long.)

POINTS TO REMEMBER

- You have repressed parts of your original True Self in order to be acceptable to your caretakers and society. These repressed parts are called the Lost Self.

- To fill the void created by repressing these Lost Self parts and to protect you from further injury from inadequate nurturing, you developed a False Self, an alias that you hope is more acceptable to your caretakers and society.

- Some of the traits that you develop as part of your False Self are also perceived as negative by your caretakers and society. You cannot get rid of these traits because you created them to protect yourself, so we deny them, creating a Disowned Self.

- Recovery of your True Self through Self-Integration is essential to your experience of genuine aliveness and to the creation of a conscious marriage free of the conflicts generated by annexing your Lost Self and projecting your Disowned Self onto your partner.

- Chronic criticisms and complaints about each other can be a rich source of healing toward Self-Integration.

REVIEW QUESTIONS

How are we wounded in the process of socialization?

How does your False Self perpetuate your Childhood Wound? (For example, how does a person who has become a strong and independent "tough guy" perpetuate the pain of not receiving enough affection as a child?)

How can we use our chronic criticisms and complaints about our partners, and his or hers of us, to help us achieve Self-Integration?

BETWEEN-SESSION ASSIGNMENTS

1. If you did not do the True Self exercise during the session, do it in the next day or two. You can do it individually.
2. Once a day, visualize yourself as your True Self. Reread your notes the first few times to help you access what you see, hear, and feel as your True Self. You can do this visualization by bringing your True Self to mind for a moment; it does not need to take a lot of time.
3. Begin to develop your True Self by expressing the one new behavior you chose to engage in this week.
4. Review the "Theory" section of Session 5, pages 82–85. In *Getting the Love You Want,* review Chapter 10, "Defining Your Curriculum," and Chapter 12, "Portrait of Two Marriages."
5. Continue:
   - Replace all criticisms, conflicts, disagreements, or fights with the Container Transaction or the Container Exercise.
   - Practice the Container Exercise at least once or twice this week with moderate Frustrations. Alternate roles and days so you play Sender and Receiver at least once each. Have a brief Couple's Dialogue after each Container Exercise to share your feelings and thoughts. Follow along in your Study Guide as you practice. If you practice this exercise regularly for three weeks, you will be able to easily contain the high voltage when it comes along. As Sender, focus on owning your communication by using "I" language. As Receiver, focus on listening with empathy, care, and compassion and visualizing your partner as a wounded child.
   - Add to any of your lists as new thoughts occur to you. Inform your partner of additions that apply to him or her.
   - Grant your partner at least one new easy Behavior Change Request this week. Note the date it is granted on the form in the Appendix, pages 263–266.

- Do at least one high-energy Fun activity with your partner every day this week.
- Give your partner another Surprise at an unexpected time this week, and enjoy his or her response. Be sure to record the date you gave the surprise. Record Surprises received from you partner, with dates.
- Give you partner at least one Caring Behavior every day this week.
- Before Session 12, have a Couple's Dialogue about the Exits you have closed or reduced so far, and choose at least one more exit to close or reduce.
- Close or reduce the Exit(s) you agreed upon.
- One day this week, write down three things that your partner does that please you (separate from granted Behavior Change Requests, Caring Behaviors, Surprises, and Fun), and share them with him or her at the end of the day. Record them in the Appendix, pages 240–242. Include the date in column 1.
- Visualize your partner as a wounded child, especially in conflict situations and when he or she behaves in ways that frustrate you.
- Use the Couple's Dialogue as a habitual part of your communication with your partner.
- Read your Mutual Relationship Vision together at least once before Session 12.

6. **Remember:**
   - Give your partner the gifts of Caring Behaviors, Surprises, and granting Behavior Change Requests regardless of how you feel about your partner and regardless of how many gifts your partner gives you.
   - Acknowledge your partner appreciatively for each gift he or she gives you—Behavior Change Requests, Surprises, Caring Behaviors, and any others.
   - Engage in high-energy Fun activities on a daily basis.
   - Continue, even if you feel resistance to any of the exercises, to take the risk of doing something new and therefore perhaps uncomfortable, in order to create your conscious marriage. Remember, the more difficult a particular exercise seems to you, the more potential it contains for growth.

Visualization of Love

REVIEW in *The New Couples' Study Guide*
Theory section, Session 10.

REVIEW in *Getting the Love You Want*
Chapter 10, "Defining Your Curriculum," and Chapter 12, "Portrait of Two Marriages."

TIME FRAME:
1 hour and 30 minutes.

PART I Container Days

OBJECTIVES

- Greatly increase the emotional safety between you and your partner.

- Safely allow deeper feelings to emerge in your relationship.

- Further reduce your fear of anger.

THEORY

A *Container Day* is the Container Transaction process stretched over a 24-hour period. One partner expresses for a full day, and the other partner contains. On a Container Day, Container Transactions do not require appointments. The Sender has a standing appointment to do them all day. (Note: Container Exercises for highly charged feelings *do* still require appointments.)

Extending the healing effect of a Containment Process over a longer period of time allows our deepest feelings to emerge and further reduces our fear of anger. We learn to integrate the expression of anger and frustration with all the other feelings that we express in the course of everyday dialogue. As our fear of anger decreases, our relationship becomes safer, and our intimacy is deepened. Emotional safety is the key to a relationship between passionate friends in a Conscious Marriage.

A safe and healthy environment, or Container, for our feelings involves appropriate expression and appropriate reception within agreed-upon parameters. A basic dynamic of all the containment processes is that only one partner expresses at a time. Healing can occur only if expressed feelings are fully received and the Receiver is not reactive to what is expressed. On a Container Day, the Receiver/Container listens, Mirrors, Validates, and Empathizes all day without responding with communications of his or her own about the feelings of anger or frustration voiced by the Sender. The Sender simply expresses himself or herself, honoring the safety guidelines, all day.

Container Days drastically increase the safety for us and our partners to express frustrations and negative feelings. Few of us have ever been in an environment in which this was possible without fear of unpleasant consequences. As children, most of us had to suppress our negative feelings because of lack of support for them from our parents. Even the best parents had difficulty being empathic when we were frustrated, especially when our frustrations were directed at them. Having no way to discharge pent-up painful feelings, we either acted them out with disruptive behavior for which we were punished, or we suppressed our impulses and replaced them with nice behavior for which we were rewarded. Either choice left us with blocked and denied pain that influences every interaction with our partner. Container Days create an environment in which our previously unacceptable feelings can be fully, safely expressed. Like the river that is finally, permanently released from the dam, our life force can flow freely, nourishing and sustaining us in every part of our lives.

CONTAINER DAYS
AGREEMENTS AND GUIDELINES

Safety Agreements

- Create a safe environment for yourself and your partner.
- Both partners stay fully present until each process is completed.
- Neither partner causes any bodily harm to himself or herself or to his or her partner.
- Neither partner destroys any property.

Guidelines for Sender

- You are free to express any of your Frustrations at any time, all day long. Your complaints may be directed at your partner or may be about a third party or situation.
- You may make Behavior Change Requests after you have expressed a Frustration.
- On a Container Day, Container Transactions do not require appointments—you have a standing appointment to do them all day. Container Exercises for highly charged feelings *do* still require appointments.
- Create safety when you express your feelings.
  - As much as possible, use "I" language that describes your experience and feelings.
  - Describe the behaviors that are upsetting to you.
  - Do *not* call your partner abusive names or criticize his or her character or motivation.

Guidelines for Receiver/Container

- Listen at any time during the day to all of your partner's complaints and frustrations.
- Mirror, Validate, and Empathize with all of your partner's communications of Frustration.
- Do *not* respond.
- Grant requests for Container Exercises as soon as possible, preferably immediately.
- Create safety by anchoring yourself in containment mode all day.
  - Visualize your partner as a wounded child.
  - Remember that your partner's feelings are rooted in his or her childhood. Your actions have triggered your partner into his or her Childhood Wound, but you are not the original cause of the hurt and therefore not the target.
  - Listen to your partner with empathy, care, and compassion.
  - *Receive* your partner's communication, rather than responding to it.

EXERCISE

Container Days

    Δ   Read through the exercise now, and begin alternating Container Days tomorrow.

    Δ   A Container Day is essentially the Container Transaction stretched over a 24-hour period.

STEP 1.

Carefully read the "Container Days Agreements and Guidelines" on pages 225–226.

STEP 2.

Decide who will be the Sender and who will be the Receiver/Container on the first day (tomorrow).

STEP 3.

Alternate roles daily for three months. If you like, take off one day per week.

- Refer to the instructions for the Container Transaction in Session 10, Steps 7 through 13 (pages 181–182), if you need to.

PART 2 Visualization of Love

OBJECTIVE

- Anchor and amplify the positive changes you have been making in your relationship.

THEORY

Love is a decision and an attitude expressed as an unconditional behavior. A loving attitude values the total welfare of another person as equal in value to your own welfare. The decision to love is to express that value as an unconditional behavior. Feeling attends love, but it does not constitute it, nor is it a part of its essence. But when feelings are present, the experience of love is complete.

This kind of love is not natural to us. Our natural directives are to preserve our lives, to seek the genuine experience of full aliveness, and to express our life energy in creative ways. When we love, as defined above, we transcend these directives. We turn our life energy away from ourselves and toward the enhancement of the life energy of another person. We become open to this other person, which we call intimacy, and we include his or her psychological healing and spiritual wholeness in our agenda.

This kind of love involves skills that we must learn. As children, we expected to be loved. In order to be loved as adults, we must become lovers. To learn to love in this way, we must suspend our natural drive to get love for ourselves. Most of us are looking for love; we are not looking for someone to love. Developing the skills presented in this book will help you transcend your natural interest in your own self-preservation to include another.

Two of the most valuable skills for creating change are visualization and intention. To visualize means to create and hold an image in your mind until it becomes your experience. To intend is to place an order to the universe, as you would in a restaurant, for something you want to receive. Both processes are simple and require only a minute or two. To visualize something, we bring to mind what it is we imagine we will see, hear, and feel in the future, when we have what it is we want to create. To intend something, we speak what it is we want to create, simply and specifically, beginning with the words "I intend . . ."

We can create only what we can imagine. And what we imagine, we can create. The principle of selective perception says that whatever we focus our thoughts upon we attract to us. When we focus our thoughts positively on what we want, like a radio tuned to a certain frequency, those things come to us. Visualize and intend what you want, and just as you order the pasta primavera at your favorite restaurant, go about your business expecting that what you order will come to you. You can visualize, intend, and get the love you want.

EXERCISE

Visualization and Intention of Love (Guided Visualization)

Suggested time: 30 minutes.

△   Read one sentence at a time. Complete the action described in the sentence, then move on to the next.

△   Do this exercise individually, reading to yourself and moving at your own pace.

△   This exercise is to become a daily meditation.

STEP 1.
Reread the description of your partner's Childhood Wound from Session 4, pages 76–77.

STEP 2.
Reread your partner's Behavior Change Requests in the Appendix of your Study Guide. Recall any other behaviors your partner needs from you to heal his or her Childhood Wound.

Visualization of Love

STEP 3.
Close your eyes, and take three deep breaths to relax.

STEP 4.
As you relax and continue to breathe, see your partner as a whole, spiritual being who has been wounded in the ways you now know about.

STEP 5.
Hold this image of your partner in your mind, and imagine that your love is healing your partner's wounds.

- Imagine yourself giving your partner some of the exact behaviors he or she needs to heal his or her wound.

STEP 6.

Imagine the energy of love that you are sending your partner coming back to you and healing your wound.

- Imagine that this energy flows back and forth between you in a continuous oscillation.

STEP 7.

As you continue to breathe and relax, see your partner as a healed and whole person without his or her Childhood Wound.

STEP 8.

Imagine yourself and your partner embraced by a warm, golden light, experiencing intense feelings of closeness and excitement.

STEP 9.

Imagine that this beam of light is your love being sent to your partner.

- Clearly identify at least one thing you see as you and your partner are bathed in this golden light of love.
- Clearly identify at least one thing you hear around you as you are embraced by this light.
- Clearly identify at least one thing you feel inside this light that is your love.

STEP 10.

As you breathe, hold the experience for 30 seconds.

Intention of Love

STEP 11.

With your eyes still closed and staying in your experience of golden light with your partner, simply phrase your experience as an intention. Clearly speak it, aloud or silently.

For example: "I intend to see my partner smiling as he or she looks at me with love shining in her or his eyes. I intend to hear a beautiful, calm silence around us. I intend to feel liberated and loved—warm, tingly, and open." Or: "I intend to love and honor my partner fully, deeply, and openly, with every part of my being, as I love and honor myself the same way."

- Start each sentence, if you use more than one, with the words "I intend . . ."

STEP 12.
Open your eyes, and continue with your daily activities.

STEP 13.
Do this exercise (Steps 3 through 12 only) three times a day for three months.

- Once you are familiar with this exercise, it should take only a minute or two to close your eyes; visualize your partner; send him or her and yourself love; see your partner as a whole person without his or her Childhood Wound; anchor into what you see, hear, and feel inside the golden light of your healing love; and speak your simple intention, aloud or silently.
- Once you have created an intention, you may continue to use it as long as it is meaningful to you.
- Feel free to change and modify your visualization and intention to keep them current and meaningful to you.

STEP 14.
On the following worksheet, note what you see, hear, and feel in the golden light of love with your partner, and write your simple Statement of Intention toward creating that love.

VISUALIZATION OF LOVE

In the golden light of love with my partner:

I see _____

_____

_____

I hear _____

_____

_____

I feel _____

_____

_____

STATEMENT OF INTENTION

I intend _____

_____

_____

_____

_____

_____

STEP 15.
Reread the Points to Remember together now.

STEP 16.
Answer the Review Questions together, noting the answers in the spaces provided.

STEP 17.
Read the Post-Session Assignments, on pages 236–238.

- The recommended practice times—for example, visualizing and intending your love three times a day for three months or practicing the Container Exercise regularly for three weeks—are intended to help you integrate these new behaviors until they become spontaneous. Once each new behavior has been integrated into your relationship, simply use it as it is appropriate.

POINTS TO REMEMBER

- When we allow ourselves and our partners full, open expression of previously unacceptable feelings, we increase our capacity for intimacy and joyous aliveness.

- Love is a decision.

- Love is an attitude expressed as an unconditional behavior which may be attended by feelings.

- Love involves skills that have to be learned.

- When we love, we transcend our interest in our own self-preservation and direct our life energy toward the total welfare of another.

REVIEW QUESTIONS

What is visualization?

What is intention?

What is the principle of selective perception, and how can we use it to help create our conscious marriage?

POST-SESSION ASSIGNMENTS

1. Begin alternating Container Days tomorrow.
2. Visualize and intend your love for your partner for one or two minutes, three times a day.
3. Review your Mutual Relationship Vision together, and take time to make any additions you may have. Use the Couple's Dialogue, if necessary. If there are additions you cannot agree upon, leave them off your Mutual Relationship Vision, and include them on your Behavior Change Request list in the Appendix, pages 254–257.
4. Practice the Container Exercise at least twice with moderate frustrations. Play Sender and Receiver at least once each.
5. After you feel comfortable with this process, select a bigger frustration. Be sure to stay in process. If you feel uncomfortable with this process, please contact an Imago therapist for assistance. Call (800) 729-1121, and ask for a referral, or log onto ImagoRelationships.org.
6. Continue:
   - Use the Couple's Dialogue as a habitual part of your communication with your partner.
   - Visualize your partner as a wounded child in conflict situations and when he or she behaves in ways that frustrate you.
   - Review your Exits in a Couple's Dialogue at least every other week, and continue to close or reduce them until they are all closed or reduced.
   - Give Caring Behaviors to your partner on a daily basis.
   - Give Surprises at unexpected times once a week or no less than once a month. Continue to keep track of Surprises given and received, if you like.
   - Do at least one high-energy Fun activity with your partner every day.
   - Translate your Frustrations into requests for specific, positively expressed behavior changes.
   - Grant Behavior Change Requests on a weekly basis. Commit to at least one a week until Stretching to meet your partner's needs becomes spontaneous and effortless.
   - Replace all criticisms, conflicts, disagreements, or fights with the Container Transaction or the Container Exercise.
   - Once a day, take a moment to visualize yourself as your True Self.
   - Develop your True Self by Stretching into a new behavior each week.

- Alternate Container Days for three months.
- Visualize and intend your love for your partner for one or two minutes, three times a day, for three months, thereafter once a day.
- Add to any of your lists as new thoughts occur to you. Inform your partner of additions that apply to him or her.

7. **Periodically:**
   - Review your Mutual Relationship Vision, adding to it if you wish.
   - Keep track of three things that your partner does in a day that please you, and share them with him or her at the end of the day.
   - Review your Exits, closing or reducing any that are open.
   - Alternate Container Days.

8. **Remember:**
   - As Sender, own your communication by using "I" language.
   - As Receiver, focus on listening with empathy, care, and compassion and on visualizing your partner as a wounded child.
   - Examine each criticism you have of your partner for possible projection.
   - Consider each criticism from your partner as a possible source of information about yourself.
   - Work from the easiest to the most difficult as you give your partner gifts of behavior, so that you experience incremental success.
   - Remind yourself that each time you Stretch into a new behavior, you are opening up to new levels of experience and weakening archaic defenses that limit your being fully alive, as well as contributing to the healing process of your partner.
   - Give your partner the gifts of Caring Behaviors, Surprises, high-energy Fun activities, and granting Behavior Change Requests regardless of how you feel about your partner and regardless of how many gifts your partner gives you.
   - Acknowledge your partner appreciatively for each gift he or she gives you (Behavior Change Requests, Surprises, Caring Behaviors, and any others).
   - Continue, even if you feel resistance to any of the exercises, to take the risk of doing something new and therefore perhaps uncomfortable, in order to create your conscious marriage. Remember, the more difficult a particular exercise seems to you, the more potential it contains for growth.

9. **For the rest of your life:**
   - Visualize your partner daily as a gift to you.
   - Give your partner a gift daily.
   - Express appreciation that your partner is in your life.
   - See your partner's needs as an opportunity for you to grow in the exact ways that will lead you to the recovery of your own original wholeness.

Congratulations! You are on your way to a Conscious Marriage.

APPENDIX

TODAY YOU PLEASED ME BY . . .

1 Date	2 Positive Behavior
	1.
	2.
	3.
	1.
	2.
	3.
	1.
	2.
	3.
	1.
	2.
	3.
	1.
	2.
	3.
	1.
	2.
	3.

1 Date	2 Positive Behavior
	1.
	2.
	3.
	1.
	2.
	3.
	1.
	2.
	3.
	1.
	2.
	3.
	1.
	2.
	3.
	1.
	2.
	3.

1 Date	2 Positive Behavior
	1.
	2.
	3.
	1.
	2.
	3.
	1.
	2.
	3.
	1.
	2.
	3.
	1.
	2.
	3.
	1.
	2.
	3.

AGREEMENT TO CLOSE EXITS

Starting this week, _____ (date), I agree to

reserve more time and energy for our relationship. Specifically, I agree to:

Signed, _____ (your signature)

- -

AGREEMENT TO CLOSE EXITS

Starting this week, _____ (date), I agree to

reserve more time and energy for our relationship. Specifically, I agree to:

Signed, _____ (your signature)

AGREEMENT TO CLOSE EXITS

Starting this week, _____ (date), I agree to

reserve more time and energy for our relationship. Specifically, I agree to:

Signed, _____ (your signature)

- -

AGREEMENT TO CLOSE EXITS

Starting this week, _____ (date), I agree to

reserve more time and energy for our relationship. Specifically, I agree to:

Signed, _____ (your signature)

AGREEMENT TO CLOSE EXITS

Starting this week, _____ (date), I agree to

reserve more time and energy for our relationship. Specifically, I agree to:

Signed, _____ (your signature)

- -

AGREEMENT TO CLOSE EXITS

Starting this week, _____ (date), I agree to

reserve more time and energy for our relationship. Specifically, I agree to:

Signed, _____ (your signature)

AGREEMENT TO CLOSE EXITS

Starting this week, _____ (date), I agree to

reserve more time and energy for our relationship. Specifically, I agree to:

Signed, _____ (your signature)

- -

AGREEMENT TO CLOSE EXITS

Starting this week, _____ (date), I agree to

reserve more time and energy for our relationship. Specifically, I agree to:

Signed, _____ (your signature)

AGREEMENT TO CLOSE EXITS

Starting this week, _____ (date), I agree to

reserve more time and energy for our relationship. Specifically, I agree to:

Signed, _____ (your signature)

- -

AGREEMENT TO CLOSE EXITS

Starting this week, _____ (date), I agree to

reserve more time and energy for our relationship. Specifically, I agree to:

Signed, _____ (your signature)

AGREEMENT TO CLOSE EXITS

Starting this week, _____ (date), I agree to

reserve more time and energy for our relationship. Specifically, I agree to:

Signed, _____ (your signature)

- -

AGREEMENT TO CLOSE EXITS

Starting this week, _____ (date), I agree to

reserve more time and energy for our relationship. Specifically, I agree to:

Signed, _____ (your signature)

CARING BEHAVIORS FOR MY PARTNER

Importance to my partner	Caring Behavior

CARING BEHAVIORS FOR MY PARTNER

Importance to my partner	Caring Behavior

CARING BEHAVIORS FOR MY PARTNER

Importance to my partner	Caring Behavior

TRANSLATING A FRUSTRATION INTO A
BEHAVIOR CHANGE REQUEST

When you (Frustrating Behavior, K): _____

_____

I feel (corresponding Feeling, L): _____

Then I react by (corresponding Reaction, M): _____

_____

To hide my fear of (corresponding Fear, N): _____

I want (corresponding Desire): _____

_____

(State the corresponding Behavior Change Request): _____

_____

TRANSLATING A FRUSTRATION INTO A
BEHAVIOR CHANGE REQUEST

When you (Frustrating Behavior, K): _____

_____

I feel (corresponding Feeling, L): _____

Then I react by (corresponding Reaction, M): _____

_____

To hide my fear of (corresponding Fear, N): _____

I want (corresponding Desire): _____

_____

(State the corresponding Behavior Change Request): _____

_____

TRANSLATING A FRUSTRATION INTO A
BEHAVIOR CHANGE REQUEST

When you (Frustrating Behavior, K): _____

_____

I feel (corresponding Feeling, L): _____

Then I react by (corresponding Reaction, M): _____

_____

To hide my fear of (corresponding Fear, N): _____

I want (corresponding Desire): _____

_____

(State the corresponding Behavior Change Request): _____

_____

- -

TRANSLATING A FRUSTRATION INTO A
BEHAVIOR CHANGE REQUEST

When you (Frustrating Behavior, K): _____

_____

I feel (corresponding Feeling, L): _____

Then I react by (corresponding Reaction, M): _____

_____

To hide my fear of (corresponding Fear, N): _____

I want (corresponding Desire): _____

_____

(State the corresponding Behavior Change Request): _____

_____

MY PARTNER'S BEHAVIOR CHANGE REQUESTS

This list of Behavior Change Requests is the ongoing
curriculum of my relationship.

Importance to my partner	Requested Behavior Change	Date granted

MY PARTNER'S BEHAVIOR CHANGE REQUESTS

This list of Behavior Change Requests is the ongoing curriculum of my relationship.

Importance to my partner	Requested Behavior Change	Date granted

MY PARTNER'S BEHAVIOR CHANGE REQUESTS

This list of Behavior Change Requests is the ongoing
curriculum of my relationship.

Importance to my partner	Requested Behavior Change	Date granted

MY PARTNER'S BEHAVIOR CHANGE REQUESTS

This list of Behavior Change Requests is the ongoing
curriculum of my relationship.

Importance to my partner	Requested Behavior Change	Date granted

CONTAINER EXERCISE
Sample

Mitch: *I'm angry, and I would like to make an appointment to express that with you. When can we do that?*

Elaine: *How angry are you?*

Mitch: *I'm pretty angry.*

Elaine: *Okay, let me call Sarah and tell her I'll speak to her tomorrow instead of tonight, and then I'll be ready, okay?*

Mitch: *Okay.*

(A few minutes later.)

Elaine: *Okay, I'm ready to hear you.*

Mitch: *I'm mad at the way you asked me to clean up my stuff.*

Elaine: *You didn't like the way I just asked you to clean up. It made you mad. Did I hear you correctly?*

Mitch: *Yeah.*

Elaine: *Okay. I get that I made you mad. I imagine it doesn't feel good to have me remind you to clean up.*

Mitch: *It makes me so mad when you judge my sense of order by yours and make me wrong for the way I do things. Every time you ask me to clean something up, I feel as if you are patronizing me or you have an attitude about it, as if I'm a bad boy or something. Or I "make a mess" just to bug you. Or I don't care. I do care. I just have a different sense of order from yours, and it really gets me when you don't honor that. I want to be able to leave my things the way I want them and clean them up or move them around when I want to, not when you want me to. So I hate having to clean up on your say-so at all. And on top of that, and maybe even more to the point, I really don't like the way you ask me to do things like that. It feels like every female in the world accusing every male in the world of being a slob. Actually, it feels like my mother accusing me of being a slob . . . or bad . . . or something like that. She used to really yell at me when she wanted me to clean up. My father, too. He never could have any space of his own to have his own things in, undisturbed. My mother wanted everything looking like some magazine. As if nobody lived there. I hate that. I guess I just want to feel as if I live here. As if there's space for me to do what I want, when I want. When you talk to me like that, I get so angry, I react by wanting to never clean up just to spite you. Let's see, I guess I should rephrase that sentence: I react to hide my fear of not having any space for me. I guess that's a fear of being dominated or of being invisible or unimportant. I like my mess. I don't want to be a slob, but I want to have creative disarray around me. It helps me think.* (Mitch is silent for a while.) *So I need us to have some agreements about this.*

Elaine: *Can we review to make sure I heard all the important points?*

Mitch: *Okay. I don't like your attitude and tone of voice when you ask me to clean up. I feel disrespected and discounted.*

Elaine: *You feel I am talking down to you and somehow not allowing you to have your own space. Did I hear you right?*

Mitch: *Yes. Definitely, we don't have clear territory agreements. The other major point is that I want you to honor my sense of order. I really don't like feeling judged because I'm different from you.*

Elaine: *You want me to respect your sense of order and stop trying to make you like me. Is that it?*

Mitch: *Yes!!! That sounds good. I guess that would be my desire. Actually, I guess the deepest-level desire is that I want to feel as if I have equal space to occupy as I want to. (Pause.) So, how could you satisfy that desire? . . . I would like to make some very clear agreements about my space that I never have to clean up if I don't want to and space that is yours that I can't ever leave a mess in, and make some really clear agreements about the common space in between. I want to decide together what "clean" looks like in the living room. I want it to be okay if it looks a little more lived-in. I would like to be able to leave what I am reading on the coffee table. I would like that to be part of the "perfect picture" of our living room. In terms of the way you talk to me about cleaning up, if I have made an agreement to clean that I am not honoring—I've spaced it out or I'm avoiding it or whatever—when you remind me to clean up, I would like you to say, "Mitch, I am doing as you asked and reminding you about your agreement to pick up your stuff in the living room." Or whatever . . . like that. First you say, "I am doing as you asked and reminding you. And I want your tone of voice when you remind me to be very neutral or even loving if you can manage it.*

Elaine: *When would it be okay to remind you? The day before? An hour before?*

Mitch: *Good question. About a half hour before the deadline we agree on. So, I would like you to remind me a half hour before my agreed-upon deadline that you are doing as I asked and reminding me of my agreement to clean up. And I would like to negotiate a space with you this weekend sometime. Have it done by the end of the weekend. That's enough for now, I guess. If I think of any more, I'll let you know.*

Elaine: *Okay. I am more than willing to clarify our agreements about your space, my space, our space. That sounds good. And it's a bit of a stretch for me, but I will commit to being okay with your current reading being on the coffee table at any time. I am happy to watch my tone of voice and to use your sentence: "Mitch, I am doing what you asked . . ." but I'll have to think about the half hour beforehand reminder. I'll put all of these on my list, though.*

Mitch: *Okay. Thank you. Wow! That's great!* (Mitch initiates a brief, happy dance with Elaine around the living room.)

Elaine: *I guess you're finished for now. Are you?*

Mitch: *Yes.* (Mitch continues to waltz Elaine around the living room.) *Thank you for hearing me.*

Elaine: *You're welcome. Thank you for letting me know what you were feeling.*

CONTAINER EXERCISE
Sample

Janet: *Todd, I am really angry. I need a Container Exercise. How soon can we do that?*

Todd: *Right now is fine. Give me just a minute. (Todd goes into containment mode.) Okay, I'm ready to hear you.*

Janet: *I'm really mad about the way you just cut me off after asking me to tell you what I felt about last night's discussion.*

Todd: *You are angry with me for interrupting you when you were talking. Is that it?*

Janet: *Yes, almost. I don't like it anytime when you interrupt me, but right now I'm even more upset because you asked me to tell you how I felt, and then you didn't listen.*

Todd: *You are angry with me for interrupting you when you were talking, especially because I asked you to tell me how you felt about our talk last night.*

Janet: *Yes!*

Todd: *I can see that it really upsets you that I interrupted you. I imagine that must make you feel as if I don't care about what you have to say.*

Janet: *I really hate it when you don't listen to me. When I am telling you how I feel about anything, especially about something important like our talk last night, I need you to hear me out—without discussion—until I am through. Can you mirror that for me?*

Todd: *You need me to sit and wait until you are done before I can talk, especially when you are talking about something important. Did I hear you correctly?*

Janet: *Not exactly. I need you to listen to me, hear what I have to say—without interruption—until I am done. I need you to listen to me, not just be waiting until it's your turn to talk.*

Todd: *Okay, you need me to just listen to you and not be thinking about what I want to say until you are done. Then I can talk. How's that?*

Janet: *That's pretty good. I guess I'm trying to say that I want you to be interested in what I have to say, I want listening to me to be an active, enjoyable thing for you. I don't want listening to have anything to do with responding. They are separate.*

Todd: *You want me to enjoy listening to what you have to say until you are completely finished and not to think about responding when I'm listening.*

Janet: *Yes! Thank you. I feel so invalidated and helpless and frustrated when you don't let me finish what I am saying. As if I don't know how to get in there and get myself heard. I feel you are impatient with what I have to say. And it makes me so mad because I don't think I should have to fight to be heard. I don't like people talking at once. I feel as if I'm in a screaming match. I know in your family you were much more casual about who talked when, but for me, I feel brutalized when you don't leave me space to talk. I want to know that you really care about what I say and that you hear me and that you value what I say even if it's different from what you might say. Especially when it's different. You don't have to agree with me, but I need you to value what I think and feel as if it is just as valid as what you think and feel. Because it is! When you interrupt me to tell me what you think, after asking me to tell you how I feel, I feel as if you think you are right. As if whatever you are think-ing or feeling is better than what I think or feel. And as if you think my opinion is stupid and you don't even want to hear it. That really gets me, especially when you ask to hear it. I want you to mirror the part about valuing—honoring—the differ-ences in what we think and feel.*

Todd: *Okay, let's see. When I interrupt you, you feel as if I don't value what you feel or think and as if I think my opinion is better than yours. Right so far?*

Janet: *Yes.*

Todd: *All right. And you want me to think that your opinion is just as valid as mine, even or especially when it's different from mine.*

Janet: *Yes, I want you to think and feel that.*

Todd: *You want me to think and feel that your opinion is just as valid as mine, even when it is different from mine.*

Janet: *Yes.* (Silence for a while.)

Todd: *Can I ask you a question about this?*

Janet: *Yes.*

Todd: *Does this remind you of anything in your childhood—your feelings about me inter-rupting you?*

Janet: *Yeah, that's good. . . . yes, it does. My dad never had enough time or patience to hear me out. I always had to give him the abbreviated version of my feelings or thoughts. And I always felt that if I didn't get it out fast enough, he would just cut me off. And he did! He used to jump in there, right as I was getting into what I was saying, and say, "Cut to the chase, Jan. I don't have all day." And when he was listening, I could see that he was impatient if I gave him any more than the barest essential facts. And then he wondered why he never knew what any of us was up to and why we always told him last. Oh, that still frustrates me so much! I felt like saying, "Shut up and lis-ten! And then you'll know what your kids are doing and thinking and feeling!" Like, "Don't you care?!" Huh. I guess I really felt as if he didn't care what we were feeling. That hurt.* (Janet cries a little for a while.) *So I really need to know that you care about what's going on with me—what I feel and think. I really need you to honor and value my feelings and thoughts by listening attentively to me until I am through with what I am saying. This goes for anytime, but especially when you ask me to tell you and when we're talking about really important stuff like last night. Can you mirror that?*

Todd: *Sure! You need to know that I care about what's going on with you, and I can show you that I do by really listening openly and patiently to everything you have to say, especially when we are talking about something important or when I have asked you to tell me what you think.*

Janet: *Yeah, you got that good! Thanks. So, specifically, whenever you ask me to tell you what I think or feel, I want you to wait to respond until I tell you I am done. And I want you to listen to me when I am talking, without thinking about what you will say when it is your turn. I will give you all the time you want to formulate and express your response. And if I don't, nail me! Also, if we are in discussion and you are not clear about whether I've finished my thought or not, because I don't want to have to rush or be cut off, ask me if I'm done. Actually, I would like our whole communication process, especially about important things, to slow down a little, so we both feel we can fully express ourselves and be heard. Maybe we need to use a Container Exercise format for important discussions, even if we're not angry—where we do the Sender/Receiver thing and really hear each other. I would like that. To be able to ask for it. And, of course, for you to ask for it if you need it. Okay, I'm done.*

Todd: *Thanks for telling me! Okay, let me just clarify your requests. When I ask you to tell me what you think or feel, you want me to wait until you are done before I even formulate my response; and you will tell me when you are done, as you just did.*

Janet: *Yup.*

Todd: *You want me to ask if you are finished if I'm not clear that you are. And you would like to be able to ask for a Container Exercise format for important discussions. I'm not sure what you mean by that.*

Janet: *I just mean doing the "explosion" part, actually, where the Sender gets to talk until they are done and to ask for Mirroring during or after. That's all I mean.*

Todd: *Okay. Well, I can agree to ask you if you are done before I start talking. I can't promise right now not to be thinking of my response—that just comes; I don't know how to control it. I'll write it down, though. And I would be willing to do the Container Exercise explosion thing, with the Mirroring during important discussions.*

Janet: *Thank you for hearing me so well. And for being willing to ask me if I'm done and being willing to do the explosion/Mirroring thing.*

Todd: *You are welcome, my sweetheart. Are you finished for now?*

Janet: *Yes, I really am. How about a big hug and then maybe a bike ride, just up the hill or something?*

Todd: *Sounds perfect!*

Index to Exercises

Index to Exercises

BY INSTRUCTIONS

About Imago Relationship Therapy

Imago Relationship Therapy is a process that helps couples use their relationship for healing and growth. Its goal is to help intimate partners understand that the unconscious purpose of committed couplehood is to finish childhood and shows them how to transform inevitable conflict into connection, thereby creating the relationship of their dreams. The Imago Process is taught by over 2,000 therapists in twenty-one countries and is practiced by millions of couples worldwide.

For information on Imago resources, please go to the website www.imagorelationships.org or call 800-729-1121 for information on workshops, seminars, other books, audio and video tapes, a list of Imago therapists, and reference to an international couples support organization called Imago Couples International.

About the Authors

Harville Hendrix, Ph.D., in partnership with his wife, Helen LaKelly Hunt, Ph.D., created Imago Relationship Therapy. They are co-founders, with other Imago therapists, of Imago Relationships International, an international non-profit organization that offers training, support, and promotion of the work of 2,000 Imago therapists in twenty-one countries. Both lecture and offer workshops on intimate relationships internationally and have together authored six books. Harville wrote *Getting the Love You Want: A Guide for Couples* and *Keeping the Love You Find: A Personal Guide,* both bestsellers, and is the co-author, with Helen, of *Giving the Love that Heals: A Guide for Parents,* also a bestseller, and three meditation books: *The Couples Companion: Meditations and Exercises for Getting the Love You Want, The Personal Companion: Meditations and Exercises for Keeping the Love You Find,* and *The Parenting Companion: Meditations and Exercises for Giving the Love that Heals.* Their books are published in over fifty-seven languages. Harville has appeared on many national television shows (thirteen times on the Oprah Winfrey show, winning for her the "most socially redemptive" award for daytime talk shows) and radio shows, and has been written up in numerous newspapers and magazines internationally. In addition to her partnership with Harville, Helen is an author in her own right with a book called *Faith and Feminism* that will be published in 2004. For her distinguished contributions to the women's movement, she has received the Gloria Steinem Award and been inducted into the Women's Hall of Fame. They live in New Mexico and New Jersey and have six children.

THE BOOK THAT STARTED IT ALL

The bestselling guide—with more than one million copies sold—to transforming an intimate relationship into a lasting source of love and companionship

"I know of no better guide for couples who genuinely desire a maturing relationship."

—M. SCOTT PECK, AUTHOR OF *THE ROAD LESS TRAVELED*

0-8050-6895-3 • $14.00/$21.95 CAN